GLUTEN-FREE
COOKIES

50 Recipes for Cookies and Bars You Crave

LUANE KOHNKE

Photographs by STACEY CRAMP

SELLERS
PUBLISHING

Dedication

To Larry, thank you for your patience and support.

Published by Sellers Publishing, Inc.

Text copyright © 2011 Luane Kohnke
Photographs copyright © 2011 Stacey Cramp
All rights reserved.

Sellers Publishing, Inc.
161 John Roberts Road, South Portland, Maine 04106
Visit our Web site: www.sellerspublishing.com • E-mail: rsp@rsvp.com

ISBN: 13: 978-1-4351-5223-6
Library of Congress Control Number: 2010933892

Printed and bound in China.

Contents

Foreword 4

Introduction 5

Welcome to Gluten-Free Cookie Baking 6

    Gluten-Free Basics: What Is and Isn't Gluten-Free 6

    Creating a Gluten-Free Baking Environment 14

    Luane's Gluten-Free Flour Mix 15

    Gluten-Free Cookie Basics 18

    Master Recipes 24

    Metric Conversion Charts 25

CLASSICS REVISITED .27

ESPECIALLY FOR CHILDREN 45

FRUIT DELIGHTS. 63

BARS AND SQUARES 83

MERINGUES ONLY 101

CELEBRATIONS AND SHARING 119

Sources for Ingredients 138

Resources for Celiac Disease 139

Index. 140

Foreword

Luane Kohnke's book, *Gluten-Free Cookies: From Shortbread to Snickerdoodles, Brownies to Biscotti: 50 Recipes for Cookies You Crave* is a wonderful compilation of fabulous cookie recipes for managing a delicious gluten-free lifestyle. Luane's book provides a wonderful way for both adults and children to enjoy a gluten-free diet.

Many people worldwide have adopted a gluten-free diet. For those with celiac disease, this diet can be life saving. While others simply find that the relief from gastro-intestinal or neurological symptoms makes their life much more comfortable. The human digestive system does not fully digest gluten. Gluten is the storage protein of wheat. (Rye and barley contain similar proteins and should also be omitted from a gluten-free diet.) Gluten intolerance can be traced to the fact that the human digestive system does not break down gluten as thoroughly as other proteins, leaving large amino acid fragments. In genetically predisposed people, these fragments trigger an inflammatory response in the small intestine that causes villous atrophy. This mechanism is more fully described in the book I co-authored, *Celiac Disease: A Hidden Epidemic*, published by HarperCollins.

The Celiac Disease Center at Columbia University provides comprehensive medical care for adults and pediatric patients with celiac disease, including nutrition and attention to the multiple associated conditions that occur in celiac disease. The Center is involved in the care of thousands of patients with celiac disease and gluten intolerance, providing better access to proper testing, diagnosis, treatment, and follow-up care. Celiac disease is a lifelong, unique autoimmune illness that occurs in about 1% of the population, worldwide.

Celiac disease and gluten intolerance are great examples of why we need to know what we are eating. This is something that is increasingly difficult in this day and age where food is often grown far from where we live, and is made more complicated with the prevalence of processed foods, fast foods, and food additives. Luane's book helps in that she not only provides copious amounts of information about available gluten-free ingredients, but she also provides recipes that allow everyone to make gluten-free homemade treats from scratch.

There is no doubt that resources such as this book, *Gluten-Free Cookies*, are an important adjunct to any household that is attempting to be gluten-free. I congratulate Luane on her superb effort. Read the book and enjoy the delicious gluten-free cookies!

Peter H.R. Green, MD
Professor of Clinical Medicine
Columbia University Medical Center
Director, Celiac Disease Center at Columbia University Medical Center
www.celiacdiseasecenter.org

Introduction

Cookies are one of life's greatest pleasures. They are small, handheld treats that contribute to our everyday enjoyment, our family get-togethers, and our holiday parties. The smell of cookies baking in the oven can recall happy childhood memories. The taste of an old favorite will remind us of our beloved Grandma or Mama, or of playtimes with friends. For some of us, cookies symbolize homemade goodness. They represent all that is good about life, sharing, and family. It is quite remarkable that these bite-sized treats of butter, sugar, and flour have such a strong place in our lives and can evoke such powerful memories.

For those who suffer from celiac disease or wheat allergies, however, memories of butter, sugar, and flour can be a painful experience. For many people, eliminating gluten from one's diet means eliminating food that was once enjoyed. For others, it means never experiencing foods like cookies, cakes, or breads that are made with wheat, rye, or barley flours. It is frustrating to have to decline a chocolate chip cookie or say no to a tempting brownie. It is difficult for adults who are gluten-intolerant, and even more difficult for children, when they see their friends enjoying food that they cannot have.

I have an enormous passion for baking cookies. Over the last fifteen years, I have created a large number of gluten-free cookie recipes. I have many friends and colleagues who have celiac disease or wheat allergies, or whose children do. Whenever they want a cookie recipe that is gluten-free, and delicious, I am the person they seek out. My approach is to use the freshest ingredients, with minimal substitution. The result is melt-in-your-mouth cookies that are made with unsalted butter, fresh and dried fruits, a variety of nuts, and different kinds of sugars. They are flavored with pure vanilla extract, fresh citrus zest, or various spices and other extracts.

I have always been inspired by European cookies. For this reason, I use nut flours in combination with brown rice flour to achieve a tastier cookie with a better texture than that achieved solely with rice flour. My cookies are not overly sweet, and while some may seem fancy, they are relatively easy to prepare, allowing even the most inexperienced baker to create a tasty cookie that just happens to be gluten-free.

This book contains a selection of my favorite recipes, spanning a broad spectrum of cookie styles. There is a chapter on the classics, which features chocolate chip cookies, flourless peanut butter cookies, and almond-lemon biscotti. The children's chapter includes jam thumbprints, cinnamon snickerdoodles, and a "pizza cookie" especially designed for a child's birthday celebration. Other chapters feature recipes for cookie bars, fruit-infused cookies, specialty meringues, and fancier cookies for celebrations and holidays, including a recipe for the ultimate gluten-free cookie, the French macaroon.

The goal of this cookie book is to present recipes that will enable the baker to create cookies that are, first and foremost, delicious — special treats to be enjoyed by everyone, gluten-intolerant or not. The cookie recipes in this book are designed to create the very best, tastiest cookies that just happen to be gluten-free. These cookies are not second-class. They are special handheld treats that rekindle the joy of eating cookies, bring back fond memories, and create new ones. I hope that you enjoy the recipes in this book, and that your cookies elicit the same reaction mine often do: "If you hadn't told me that this was gluten-free, I never would have known."

Happy baking!

Welcome to Gluten-Free Cookie Baking

Interest in maintaining a gluten-free diet has grown considerably over the last several years as more and more adults and children have been diagnosed with celiac disease or wheat allergies. Additionally, a gluten-free diet is sometimes recommended for children with autism. For some people, gluten-free eating is a lifestyle choice.

Baking for a gluten-free diet is slightly more challenging than regular baking. Essentially, gluten-free baking is learning to work with flours that substitute for wheat flours, which contain gluten. Gluten-free flours, such as rice flour, require the addition of xanthan gum or guar gum to give the baked product a texture and crumb similar to a wheat flour–based baked good. The dough created by the rice flour and xanthan gum mixture is stickier than wheat-flour dough, making it a bit more challenging to roll or shape. Therefore, most of the recipes in this book require that the dough mixture be chilled for 1 to 2 hours or overnight, to make it less sticky and easier to manage.

If you follow the food preparation instructions in these recipes, and practice a bit, you will become an expert at gluten-free cookie baking.

GLUTEN-FREE BASICS: What Is and Isn't Gluten-Free

Wheat, barley, and rye contain gluten. Gluten is the protein element of these grains. It gives baked goods elasticity, which contributes to structure and texture. Too much gluten makes baked goods rubbery and too little can make them too crumbly.

Gluten-free flours, such as brown rice flour, cannot develop the elasticity needed to create structure. For this reason, other ingredients, such as xanthan gum, guar gum, or tapioca flour, must be added to the gluten-free flour to create the proper texture.

Many of the gluten-free baking items that you will need are probably already in your refrigerator or on your pantry shelf. These include: nuts, fruits, sugar, salt, eggs, and butter. Pure vanilla extract is gluten-free, as are most natural extracts and spices. Most baking powders are gluten-free. Chocolate chips and baking chocolate are usually gluten-free, but always check the label to be sure.

Oats are a bit controversial. Some people ban oats from a gluten-free diet and others include them. Oats can be tolerated by many people with celiac disease, but they are sometimes processed in the same plant as wheat and therefore may be contaminated. Some gluten-free rolled oats, such as Bob's Red Mill, are certified gluten-free. They are processed in a plant where there is no possibility of cross-contamination with wheat, rye, or barley. Additionally, they are grown in fields that are dedicated to growing only oats from pedigree seeds that have not been genetically modified (non-GMO.) Some of the recipes in this book call for gluten-free rolled oats. If you have concerns about eating oats, you may prefer not to bake these recipes. However, there are still plenty of other recipes that you can enjoy.

Cookie decorating items, such as jimmies or sprinkles, are often made with wheat powder. However, colored sugars are, for the most part, safe. In general, check labels of all cookie decorating items thoroughly.

Many candies are gluten-free. Miniature candies, such as M&M's Minis, can be used to decorate gingerbread or cutout cookies. Read labels thoroughly or contact the manufacturer if you have questions.

• READING THE LABELS •

The most important principle in following a gluten-free diet is to read the labels of all products. There are two things to look for on labels: the ingredients and the processing environment.

Gluten-free product labeling is becoming more common. Currently, warnings concerning ingredients that may cause allergic reactions are listed on most packages. These include: wheat, eggs, tree nuts, peanuts, soy, milk, seafood, and shellfish. Barley and rye are not yet included on this list.

The ingredient list provides critical information about what is contained in the product. Gluten is in all varieties of wheat, barley, and rye, including derivatives of these grains, such as barley malt. Read all ingredient labels carefully. If you have any doubts about whether a product is gluten-free, contact the manufacturer for clarification. Also note any precautions concerning the processing environment, to avoid contact with ingredients that may have possible gluten contamination.

The Celiac Sprue Association (www.csaceliacs.org) annually publishes a complete listing of gluten-free products. It also provides information on businesses specializing in gluten free items, and it gives tips for living a gluten-free lifestyle. The Sources for Ingredients section of this book lists names and contact information for manufacturers of gluten-free baking ingredients.

• GLUTEN-FREE BAKING INGREDIENTS •

FLOURS

All-purpose gluten-free flour: All-purpose gluten-free flour blends, usually made with bean flours, are widely used in gluten-free cooking. I do not recommend substituting them for the brown rice flour used in these cookie recipes, however, as they will significantly alter the flavor of the cookie.

Almond flour: Almond flour is made from blanched almonds that have been finely ground. It is different from almond meal, which is usually made from whole almonds with skins. Almond flour is one of the key ingredients in most of these recipes. It has a neutral flavor, but it adds protein, fiber, nutrients, and fat to the flour mixture. You can buy almond flour or you can make your own by grinding slivered, blanched almonds in a food processor or nut chopper until they are finely ground. Store almond flour in the refrigerator or freezer to ensure maximum freshness.

Cornmeal: Cornmeal, both yellow and white, is ground corn. It adds a corn flavor and crunchy texture to baked goods. It is found in fine, medium, and coarse textures. For cookie recipes, use the finely ground meal.

Cornstarch (sometimes called cornflour): Cornstarch is a highly refined starch that is made from corn. It has a neutral flavor and is used alone or in combination with other gluten-free flours to add body and texture. Arrowroot can be substituted for cornstarch, if corn allergies exist. However, it should be used in limited amounts as it is creates a slick texture when combined with dairy products.

Guar gum: Guar gum is used throughout the food industry to improve the texture of baked goods and to thicken dairy products. It can be used interchangeably with xanthan gum in the cookie recipes in this book. *(See xanthan gum.)*

Hazelnut flour: Hazelnut flour is made from raw or toasted hazelnuts that are finely ground. It has a rich, sweet, nutty flavor. It is used in several of the cookie recipes in this book to add depth to the flavor. You can buy it pre-ground or grind it yourself in a food processor or nut chopper.

Potato starch: Potato starch is a finely textured starch made from raw white potatoes. It is commonly used at Passover and can be found in the kosher section of most grocery stores or in organic food shops. Potato starch should not be confused with potato flour, which is made from cooked potatoes, has a distinct potato flavor, and is a much heavier substance. Do not substitute potato flour for potato starch.

Rice flour (brown and white): Rice flour is the most common ingredient in gluten-free baked goods. It is ground from rice. It has a subtle flavor and somewhat sandy consistency. Several manufacturers, such as King Arthur, mill the rice to a fine powdery consistency, making it easier to work with in baked goods and reducing the gritty texture.

The recipes in this book call for brown rice flour. It is higher in protein, nutrients, fiber, and fat than white rice flour. I chose it as the base flour because it has a slightly nutty flavor. When baked, it turns a slightly darker shade of brown than white rice flour does. It should be stored in the refrigerator or freezer to maintain a long shelf life.

Tapioca flour (tapioca starch): Tapioca flour and tapioca starch are the same ingredient. They are also called manioc flour and are made by grinding the root of the cassava plant. Tapioca flour is a key ingredient in most of the recipes in this book. It adds body and texture. It can be found in many organic food shops or at online merchants.

Xanthan gum: Xanthan gum is a gluten substitute. It comes from the dried cell coat of a microorganism called *Zanthomonas campestris*. It is created in a laboratory using natural ingredients. It is needed to help gluten-free flours develop good structure during baking. It can be purchased in organic food shops or from online merchants. Only a small amount (usually 1/4 to 1/2 teaspoon) is needed in most cookie recipes. Guar gum can be substituted.

LEAVENERS

Baking powder: Baking powder consists of baking soda and a starch, most often cornstarch. Most baking powders are gluten-free, but check the label.

Baking soda: Baking soda is bicarbonate of soda. It reacts with acids in recipes to create carbon dioxide, which makes baked goods rise. Baking soda is naturally gluten-free.

Cream of tartar: Cream of tartar is used to stabilize and give more volume to beaten egg whites. It is the acidic ingredient in some brands of baking powder. It is also used to produce a creamier texture in frosting. If you don't have cream of tartar, you can substitute white vinegar in the same ratio as cream of tartar in the meringue recipes, generally 1/8 teaspoon per egg white.

Eggs: Eggs are gluten-free. They add to leavening, bind ingredients together, and add protein. Large eggs are called for in these recipes. Egg yolks, when used alone, add richness and density to a cookie. Egg whites are the basis of the meringue cookies.

SWEETENERS

Agave nectar: Agave nectar is most often produced from Blue Agave succulent plants that grow in southern Mexico. Agave nectar is sometimes used in place of honey. It is gluten-free.

Brown sugar (light and dark): Brown sugar is granulated sugar and molasses. Most brown sugar is gluten-free, but be sure your brand is made with molasses, not invert sugar, which may contain wheat or barley derivatives.

Corn syrup: Corn syrup is made from the starch of corn. It is used in baking to add volume, soften texture, and enhance flavor. Most corn syrups are gluten-free.

Granulated sugar (regular and superfine): Sugar is obtained mainly from sugarcane or sugar beets and is used in many foods. Superfine sugar is finely ground granulated sugar. Outside of the USA, it is called castor sugar. Superfine sugar is used in meringue recipes because it dissolves more quickly than regular granulated sugar. Granulated sugar is gluten-free.

Honey: Honey is a gluten-free, naturally sweet food made by bees from the nectar of flowers. Flavors of honey vary based on the nectar source. Various types and grades of honey are commercially available.

Molasses: Molasses is the viscous by-product from the processing of sugarcane or sugar beets into sugar. It is naturally gluten-free and is often used in gingerbread cookies.

Powdered sugar (confectioners' sugar): Powdered sugar is pulverized sugar and a small amount of cornstarch. Be sure cornstarch, not wheat starch, is used. Powdered sugar is usually gluten-free.

Pure maple syrup: Maple syrup is a sweetener made by boiling the sap from sugar maple and black maple trees. It is naturally gluten-free.

FLAVORINGS

Chocolate (chocolate chips and baking bars): In general, chocolate chips and baking chocolate are gluten-free. However, some chocolate products are not, because of the ingredients or the processing environment in which they are manufactured. Products containing barley malt are not gluten-free. Products that contain modified food starch, artificial colors, or artificial flavors are usually not gluten-free. Read the label carefully. If you have questions, check with the manufacturer.

Cocoa powder (unsweetened and Dutch-process): Cocoa powder provides a deep chocolate flavor and dark color to baked goods. Unsweetened cocoa can serve as leavening in recipes using baking soda. Dutch-process cocoa is unsweetened cocoa that has been treated with alkali. It works well in recipes with baking powder. For best results, use the type of cocoa specified in the recipe.

Espresso powder: Espresso powder is made from brewed, dried espresso. A small amount of espresso powder ($\frac{1}{2}$ to 1 teaspoon) enhances chocolate flavor without adding any coffee flavor. Espresso powder is gluten-free.

Extracts (almond, lemon, maple, peppermint): Most extracts that are "pure," such as pure almond, pure peppermint, pure lemon, or pure maple extract, are made from plants and are gluten-free. Most "artificial" or "imitation" extracts are not, because they usually contain a barley derivative. Read labels carefully.

Spices: Spices are aromatic substances that are used to enhance the flavor of foods. They are made from dried roots, bark, or seeds and are naturally gluten-free.

Vanilla (beans and extract): Vanilla extract is made from vanilla beans that are macerated and aged in ethyl alcohol and water for about 48 hours. Artificial or imitation vanilla extract is usually not gluten-free, as it often contains barley malt for flavoring. Only pure vanilla is gluten-free.

OTHER INGREDIENTS

Butter, milk, and cream: These dairy products are gluten-free. All contain some amount of fat, which adds flavor and texture to cookies.

Unsalted butter is used in many recipes in this book. It is either used at room temperature, cold, or melted. Different butter consistencies (soft, hard, liquid) create different cookie textures. For best results, use the style of butter specified in the recipe.

Milk refers to whole milk, and cream refers to heavy cream. Small quantities are used in some recipes. Milk and cream contain fat and protein that contribute valuable nutrients to baked goods. They also add flavor.

Fruit (fresh and dried): Fresh and dried fruits as well as fruit jams and jellies are gluten-free. Coconut is also gluten-free. Fruit adds natural sweetness to recipes and is a source of energy and nutrients. Fruit is a key ingredient in many of the recipes in this book, including an entire chapter dedicated to fruit-infused cookies.

Gelatin: Gelatin powder, unflavored and flavored, is gluten-free.

Nuts and seeds: Tree nuts, peanuts, nut butters, and seeds are all gluten-free. Many of the recipes in this book use nuts, nut butters, or nut flour as an ingredient. Nuts are one of the best sources of protein and fiber

Oil and shortening (vegetable and olive): Vegetable oil, vegetable shortening, and olive oil are gluten-free. Vegetable oil is used in some recipes to lightly grease cookie sheets or baking pans.

Vegetable shortening is a semisolid fat used in baked goods to create a crumbly texture. Virgin olive oil is pressed from ripe olives. It has a more robust flavor than vegetable oil. Vegetable shortening and virgin olive oil are used in some recipes to add fat.

White vinegar: White vinegar is distilled, clear vinegar. The distillation process removes the gluten proteins. Malt vinegar, which is not distilled, has gluten. All distilled vinegar is considered gluten-free.

• INGREDIENTS TO AVOID •

Barley flour and barley derivatives: Barley flour and barley malt are often used as additives in products to thicken them or add flavor. Barley malt is a sweetener that is often found in artificial flavorings.

Rye flour and rye derivatives: Rye flour is milled from a hardy cereal grass. It contains less gluten than all-purpose wheat flour. It is often used in combination with wheat flour.

Wheat flour and wheat derivatives: Wheat flour and its by-products are made from wheat grain. The protein in the wheat is the gluten substance. Wheat flour is used in most baked goods.

To learn more about these grains and their derivative products, see *The New Oxford Book of Food Plants* by John Vaughan and Catherine Geissler.

• INGREDIENTS TO EVALUATE •

Cookie decorating items, colored sugar, and candies: Cookie decorating items should be evaluated carefully. Most jimmies, sprinkles, and dragees contain wheat powder and should be avoided. However, gluten-free versions of some cookie decorating products can be found at some online merchants.

Colored sugars are, for the most part, safe. India Tree sugars are gluten-free, containing only sugar, food coloring, and sometimes paraffin. Check labels, however, as some colored sugars contain wheat or barley additives. Miniature candies, such as M&M's Minis, are gluten-free and can be used for decorating. Both Mars and Nestle manufacture many chocolate candies that are gluten-free. Read labels thoroughly or contact the manufacturer, if you have questions.

Oats: According to a 2008 research study published in the *Scandinavian Journal of Gastroenterology*, pure oats are safe for most people with celiac disease. Contamination during the manufacturing process is the main problem. Gluten-free rolled oats are manufactured by several companies. If you have any questions or concerns about oats, contact the manufacturer.

• GLUTEN-FREE BAKING INGREDIENTS LIST •

Flours:
All-purpose gluten-free flour
Almond flour
Cornmeal
Cornstarch
Guar gum
Hazelnut flour
Potato starch
Rice flour: brown and white
Tapioca flour (aka tapioca starch)
Xanthan gum

Flavorings:
Chocolate: chips and baking bars
    (check labels)
Cocoa powder: natural unsweetened
    and Dutch-process
Espresso powder
Other pure extracts: almond,
    peppermint, lemon, orange,
    and maple
Spices and salt
Vanilla: beans and pure extract

Leaveners:
Baking powder
Baking soda
Cream of tartar
Eggs

Other Ingredients:
Butter
Cream
Fruit: fresh and dried
Gelatin: unflavored and flavored
Milk
Nuts and seeds: tree nuts, peanuts,
    nut butters, and seeds
Oil: vegetable and olive
Vegetable shortening
White vinegar, any distilled vinegar

Sweeteners:
Agave nectar
Brown sugar: light and dark
Corn syrup
Granulated sugar: regular and superfine
Honey
Molasses
Powdered sugar
Pure maple syrup

Creating a Gluten-Free Baking Environment

It is not difficult to create a gluten-free baking environment for a single baking session, or to permanently maintain a completely gluten-free preparation and baking area.

One simple rule to follow is: "gluten-free first." If you are sharing a kitchen with food that contains gluten, gluten contamination is possible. Therefore, when baking, always prepare the gluten-free items first. This makes it less likely that equipment, such as cookie sheets and baking pans, will be contaminated by gluten crumbs.

If it is not practical to make the gluten-free items first, thoroughly wash all baking equipment, including utensils, cookie sheets, and baking pans, before using them. Otherwise, maintain and use an entirely different set of "gluten-free only" utensils and pans for gluten-free baking. As part of the food preparation process, thoroughly clean all surfaces, including countertops and cutting boards. Using a clean cloth or damp sponge, wipe down standing mixers and the exterior surfaces of food processors. It is important to remember that even a few gluten-containing crumbs can be harmful to people who have celiac disease or wheat allergies.

When rolling gluten-free cookie dough, be sure to put the dough between two sheets of wax paper before rolling. In addition to making cleanup easier, this will prevent stray crumbs on countertops or rolling pins from contaminating gluten-free cookie dough.

Many of the recipes in this book call for lining cookie sheets with parchment paper and baking pans with aluminum foil. This helps to keep cookies from sticking to pans and also adds a further layer of protection from gluten contamination.

If possible, maintain a "gluten-free only" container for your gluten-free cookies. However, if the container is also used occasionally for gluten-based products, be sure that it has been thoroughly washed and dried to minimize the possibility of gluten contamination.

Finally, never commingle gluten-free cookies and gluten-based cookies. Serve gluten-free cookies on separate plates or trays, apart from any gluten-based items. Inform people as to which cookies are gluten-free and which are not. Label serving trays, if you feel it is necessary. This will help to prevent any possible confusion or contamination of your delicious gluten-free cookies. (And if you are among gluten-consuming friends or family, encourage them to sample your gluten-free cookies. I am confident that your cookies will receive excellent reviews. After all, they will be delicious. They just happen to be gluten-free.)

Luane's Gluten-Free Flour Mix

Since I was nine years old, working next to my Mom in our farmhouse kitchen, I have enjoyed baking cookies. And, judging from the rave reviews my cookies receive from friends and family, I have achieved a measure of success as a baker. So when I became interested in gluten-free baking, my goal was to create cookies that tasted delicious, had a good texture, and looked appealing.

Any gluten-free baker will tell you that the flour blend is the foundation for all the baking goodness that follows. That is true for the recipes in this book as well. For this reason, I gave considerable time and attention to testing different flour blends before arriving at the best option for the cookie recipes in this book.

For these recipes, I tested four different gluten-free flour blends. Each flour blend was used to prepare the same shortbread cookie recipe. A gluten-based "control" cookie was also prepared, using wheat flour. The control cookie was used as the model for taste, texture, and appearance.

A panel of testers, including both gluten-tolerant and gluten-intolerant individuals, sampled the test cookies. The gluten-tolerant taste-testers also tasted the gluten-based control cookie. Testers completed written evaluations of the cookies, describing taste, texture, and appearance. They also rated the cookies on overall attractiveness. Each tester selected a favorite from among the test cookies, and documented why it was favored. Gluten-tolerant individuals compared their favorite test cookie to the control cookie, to determine how similar they were.

The four gluten-free flour blends tested were:

> **1. White rice flour blend:** A classic blend of 6 parts white rice flour, 2 parts potato starch, and 1 part tapioca flour.

> **2. Brown rice flour blend:** 6 parts brown rice flour, 2 parts potato starch, and 1 part tapioca flour.

> **3. All-purpose, premixed blend:** Bob's Red Mill All-Purpose Gluten-Free Baking Flour, containing garbanzo flour, potato starch, tapioca flour, sorghum flour, and fava flour.

> **4. Brown rice flour and almond flour blend:** Same as the brown rice flour blend above, with the addition of 2¼ parts almond flour.

I found the results of the test interesting. As an experienced baker, I know that taste, texture, and appearance are all important cookie attributes. The relative importance of each of these components varies among different people. In my flour blend evaluation, the brown rice flour and almond flour blend (Blend #4) created a preferred taste, texture, and appearance. When compared to the gluten-based wheat-flour control, it was considered to be the closest match on all criteria. The comparison to the control cookie was important to me because it indicated that this blend could create a cookie that even gluten-eaters would like.

The brown rice flour blend without the almond flour (Blend #2) was the second choice among the test panel, delivering well on taste but not as well on appearance. The white rice flour blend (Blend #1) was a close runner-up to the brown rice flour mix. Bob's Red Mill All-Purpose Gluten-Free Baking Flour (Blend #3) scored highest on appearance, but lowest on taste.

Based on the test results, I selected the brown rice flour and almond flour blend for the recipes in this book. So that the baker does not have to refer back to this section, each recipe specifies the amount of brown rice flour, potato starch, tapioca flour, and almond flour to be used.

For the occasional baking session, it doesn't make sense to premix a large quantity of this specialized gluten-free flour blend. However, if you wish to do so for convenience, sift together 6 parts brown rice flour, 2 parts potato starch, and 1 part tapioca flour, then whisk in $2\frac{1}{4}$ parts almond flour. To maintain freshness, store the flour blend in an airtight container in the refrigerator. When ready to bake, add together the amounts of brown rice flour, potato starch, tapioca flour, and almond flour used in the recipe, measure that amount of the pre-mixed flour blend, and then sift together with xanthan gum, baking soda, salt, etc., as specified in the recipe. Note that for the almond lemon biscotti recipe in this book, the almond flour proportion is larger.

If you wish to convert a favorite wheat flour–based recipe to a gluten-free recipe, conversion guidelines are provided in the table on the opposite page. Please note that the amount of xanthan gum may vary, depending on the texture of the cookie that you are creating. For example, crumbly drop cookies require less xanthan gum than cakelike brownies, even though the amounts of brown rice flour may be the same.

LUANE'S BROWN-RICE AND
ALMOND-FLOUR BLEND EQUIVALENTS

BROWN-RICE AND ALMOND-FLOUR BLEND MEASURES:					
Wheat Flour Equivalent:	Brown Rice Flour	Potato Starch	Tapioca Flour	Almond Flour	Xanthan Gum
½ cup	⅓ cup	1½ tablespoons	2½ teaspoons	2 tablespoons	⅛ to ¼ teaspoon
1 cup	⅔ cup	3 tablespoons	1 tablespoon plus 2 teaspoons	¼ cup	¼ teaspoon
1½ cups	1 cup	⅓ cup	2½ tablespoons	¼ cup plus 2 tablespoons	½ teaspoon
1¾ cups	1 cup plus 2½ tablespoons	⅓ cup plus 2¼ teaspoons	2 tablespoons plus 2¾ teaspoons	¼ cup plus 3 tablespoons	½ teaspoon

Gluten-Free Cookie Basics

Well-made cookies are perfect gems of flavor and texture. Gluten-free cookies are no exception. They require the finest baking ingredients to deliver the flavors and textures that create delicious cookies. For all of your cookie creations, use only the best-quality unsalted butter, chocolate, nuts, fruit, cocoa, brown rice flour, and extracts. The best ingredients will help you achieve the tastiest results. If dietary restrictions compel you to use margarine in place of butter, the flavor of the cookie will change, but the texture will be virtually identical.

Since baking is a bit of chemistry, it is important to accurately measure all ingredients and to follow instructions carefully. Begin by reading the recipe ingredients and noting what is needed. Also read the preparation instructions, from beginning to end, once or twice. Note the equipment needed, such as baking sheets, parchment paper, mixers, rubber spatulas, cooling racks, etc. Make note of the time that may be required for chilling the dough, or if any other special preparation is required, such as toasting nuts. Be aware that gluten-free doughs are stickier than wheat flour–based doughs and are usually chilled for 1 to 2 hours or overnight to make them easier to handle. Prep all the ingredients prior to beginning the mixing process. Anticipate what you will need and have the ingredients ready. If you do this, you will find yourself moving smoothly through the entire process of creating cookies.

Because gluten-free doughs are stickier than wheat flour doughs, the recipes in this book call for either lining the cookie sheets with parchment or lightly oiling them. Baking pans for bar cookies are usually completely lined with foil, and sometimes a parchment bottom-liner is recommended. Sometimes the pan's bottom and sides are also lightly oiled or buttered. Lining and/or oiling the pans will prevent the cookies from sticking when they are baked.

After baking, gluten-free cookies should be stored in an airtight container and consumed within a few days. Gluten-free cookies have a tendency to dry out, and they start to lose their flavor after a few days. To extend their freshness, you may want to freeze them, after double-wrapping in plastic wrap or foil and sealing them in an airtight plastic freezer bag. At serving time, thaw the amount that you plan to use.

Gluten-Free Baking Tips

1. Read recipe in advance
2. Prepare ingredients prior to mixing
3. Chill most doughs for at least 1 hour
4. Line cookie sheets with parchment
5. Store baked cookies in an airtight container

• TECHNIQUES AND TERMS •

Here are basic techniques and terms used in the recipes in this book. If you are an experienced baker, you will be familiar with them. If you are new to baking, this section is worth reading and you may want to practice the techniques.

Beating eggs: Eggs should always be at room temperature before being used in any of these recipes. Room temperature eggs achieve greater volume when being beaten. This is especially important for the egg whites used in meringue cookie recipes. Beaten eggs should be used immediately.

Chilling dough: Many of the cookie recipes in this book require chilling the dough for 1 to 2 hours, or overnight, before baking. Gluten-free doughs are sticky, and chilling makes the dough easier to work with. For some cookies, such as Five-Spice Ginger Cookies, a longer chilling time is recommended to help flavors develop fully prior to baking.

Chopping nuts: Chopping nuts can easily be done by hand, using a sharp knife or mezzaluna, or by machine, using a coffee grinder, nut chopper, or food processor fitted with a small bowl. Most recipes refer to the size of the chopped pieces as coarsely chopped, chopped, or finely chopped. These are gradations of size from large (coarse) to very small (fine).

Creaming: Creaming butter is a basic baking technique. It introduces air into the butter. Air is the foundation of the cookie's texture and structure. Using an electric mixer set at high speed, room temperature butter is beaten until it is almost white. After creaming the butter, the sugar, extracts, and eggs are usually added, in that order, and they are also beaten at high speed to add additional air and lightness to the batter.

Cutting in: Cutting in refers to using a pastry cutter or two knives to "chop" cold butter or shortening into a flour mixture. This mixes the fat into the flour mixture in small pieces. The resulting mixture will resemble flakes or coarse meal.

Dusting pans: Some of the bar cookie recipes suggest dusting the greased pans with rice flour or all-purpose gluten-free flour. Dusting is recommended so that the cookies do not stick to the pan. To dust the pan, lightly sprinkle with the gluten-free flour, tilt and tap the pan to create a light even layer of flour on the bottom of the pan, and tap out any excess flour.

Firm to touch: Many of the recipes indicate to bake until "firm to touch." This means that when the surface of the baked item is lightly touched, no indentation remains on the baked surface.

Firmly packed: Brown sugar, light and dark, as well as citrus zest are measured as firmly packed. To pack firmly means to press the ingredient into the measuring cup or spoon so that there are no gaps or air bubbles. Measures should be level.

Folding in: Folding is the process of combining a heavier ingredient, such as melted chocolate, into a lighter ingredient, such as beaten egg whites. It is best accomplished by using a rubber spatula to gently cut through the center of the ingredients and carefully turn over the batter until the mixture is homogenous. Overmixing will deflate the air that is in the batter, so when folding, take a slow and gentle approach to maintain the volume of the batter.

Greasing pans: To grease pans, lightly spray or coat with a very thin layer of vegetable oil or butter.

Grinding nut flours: Almond flour and hazelnut flour, two of the basic ingredients used throughout this book, should be finely ground. If you are making the flour yourself, use a coffee grinder, electric nut chopper, or a food processor fitted with a small bowl to grind the nuts. Nut flours should be combined with other flours by whisking with a fork or balloon whisk.

Measuring dry ingredients: Dry ingredients are measured in graduated measuring cups or spoons. Typically, the dry ingredient is added to the measuring cup by spooning it into the cup. For flour, powdered sugar, baking soda, and baking powder, it may be beneficial to stir prior to spooning to remove any lumps and to aerate the ingredient. When using a measuring spoon, you can lightly scoop the ingredient from the container. The tops should be leveled with a straightedge, such as the back edge of a table knife, to ensure an accurate quantity.

Melting chocolate: To melt chocolate, place chopped chocolate in the top bowl of a double boiler, over barely simmering water. Butter is sometimes melted with the chocolate. Do not apply too much heat. That will cause the chocolate to scorch. Also, do not allow any water to mix with the chocolate. If mixed with water, the chocolate will become hard and will need to be discarded.

Piping: Use a pastry bag that has been fitted with a ½-inch tip. If you do not have a pastry bag, a large, heavy-duty, ziplock plastic bag, with a very small opening cut in one corner, will work as well. Fill the bag, moving the batter to the tip or opening. Hold the top of the bag with your writing hand. While guiding the bag with your other hand, gently squeeze the top to move the batter through the bag opening. Pipe the batter into small mounds or ovals. Rest the bag by standing it in a tall glass. If piping frosting to decorate cookies, see the Royal Icing recipe in the Master Recipes section of this book for ideas.

Preheating oven: Cookies need to go into a hot oven to bake properly. It usually takes about 15 minutes for an oven to heat to the proper baking temperature. Don't ignore this step!

Room temperature: Many recipes in this book call for room temperature butter. Room temperature does not mean warm or melted. Butter that is room temperature will be cool in the center, and just beginning to soften. Butter and eggs should be removed from the refrigerator and allowed to reach room temperature before being used in a recipe. In a hot kitchen, they will warm to room temperature more quickly.

Sifting: Dry ingredients, such as brown rice flour, potato starch, tapioca flour, and xanthan gum, should be sifted together before being added to the batter. Sifting is the process of passing the dry ingredients through a mesh strainer to remove any lumps.

Toasting nuts: Toasting enhances the flavor of nuts. It is a simple procedure that enhances the depth and complexity of the cookie flavor. In the Master Recipes section of this book, there are instructions for toasting nuts.

Whisking: Whisking means to aerate dry ingredients or to lightly mix liquids together using a fork or a balloon whisk.

Zest: To zest is to remove the outer rind of citrus fruits in narrow strips. The outer rind of oranges, lemons, etc., contains flavorful oils that enhance the taste of baked goods. Zest should only be taken from the outer colorful layer of the rind and not from the white pith, which is bitter. Zest should be finely chopped before measuring and adding to batter. Grated rind can be substituted for zested rind.

• EQUIPMENT •

In order to make a batch of cookies, you will need some basic tools to measure, mix, shape, and bake the cookies. Gluten-free baking does not require any special equipment. If you are using equipment that is also used for gluten-based ingredients, wash everything thoroughly, and follow the guidelines noted in the Creating a Gluten-Free Baking Environment section of this book.

If you are an experienced baker, you will probably already have all of the equipment that is needed for the recipes in this book. If you are new to baking, you will need to obtain the basic bowls, spoons, measuring cups and spoons, cookie sheets or baking pans, parchment paper, and wire cooling racks. Although most recipes use cookie scoops to shape the dough, you can use your hands to roll or shape the dough.

A sifter, cookie cutters, an electric mixer, and a nut chopper are all good items to have on hand to make the cookie creation process faster and easier. Rubber spatulas for scraping bowls or folding-in ingredients are also good to have, as is an offset spatula for moving cutout cookies to the baking sheets. Cookie tins or airtight containers are recommended to keep baked cookies fresh.

Here is a list of equipment that will help you prepare the recipes in this book.

Baking pans: Baking pans are used for making bar cookies. Use sturdy aluminum pans with straight sides. They are best for conducting heat.

Brownie cutter: A brownie or bar cutter is used to score bar cookies prior to cutting. A brownie cutter has six or seven stainless steel tines attached to a straight handle. More elaborate cutters have multiple blades that cut a pan of brownies into equal-size portions in one motion.

Cookie cutters: Cookie or biscuit cutters are sturdy-rimmed cutters that come in a variety of shapes and sizes. For gluten-free cookies, which tend to have stickier dough, 1-inch to $1\frac{1}{2}$-inch tin or stainless steel cookie cutters are recommended. Plastic cutters and large cookie cutters will not work as effectively with gluten-free dough.

Cookie scoops: Cookie scoops are very useful tools. They form cookie balls of uniform shapes and sizes, and they eliminate the need to hand-roll the dough. A small scoop is #100, and #40 is a medium scoop. Many of the recipes in this book suggest using a cookie scoop.

Cookie sheets: Rimless cookie sheets are recommended for the recipes in this book, because they make it easier to remove delicate cookies to wire cooling racks. Dark, heavy-duty, insulated sheets are best to conduct heat and produce even browning. They will work best for most recipes in this book.

Double boiler: Double boilers are ideal for melting chocolate. Water is simmered in the lower pan, while ingredients that are to be melted are placed in the upper pan. If you do not have a double boiler, you can use two saucepans.

Dry measuring cups: Dry measuring cups come in graduated sizes. Their straight, even rims allow ingredients to be leveled accurately.

Electric mixer: An electric mixer is called for in most of the recipes in this book. A countertop or "stand" mixer is recommended to assist in mixing cookie dough. If you do not have a countertop mixer, a handheld electric mixer will work, although it may be tiring to use.

Food processor: Food processors are ideal for chopping and blending. If you don't have a food processor, you can get the same results using kitchen knives, a grater, or a blender.

Kitchen knives: A paring knife, utility knife, and knife with a serrated blade are basic knives that are helpful in the preparation of cookie ingredients, as well as in slicing refrigerator cookie rolls, cutting bar cookies, and slicing biscotti before the second baking.

Kitchen spoons: Stainless steel spoons and wooden mixing spoons are needed for mixing and scooping dough.

Liquid measuring cups: Liquid measuring cups should be made of heavy-duty heat-resistant glass. They should be marked with cups and ounces. If necessary, you can substitute dry-measuring cups.

Measuring spoons: Measuring spoons come in graduated sizes and are used to measure small quantities of ingredients. Standard sets usually include four or five spoons ranging from $\frac{1}{8}$ teaspoon up to 1 tablespoon. You can find special baking-focused measuring spoon sets at Williams-Sonoma or King Arthur Flour. These sets will include special measures such $1\frac{1}{2}$ tablespoons or 2 teaspoons.

Mixing bowls: For easy mixing, use bowls with high sides. Glass and ceramic bowls both work well. Bowls with lips and handles facilitate pouring.

Parchment paper: Parchment paper is essential in making gluten-free cookies. It is ovenproof paper that is used to line cookie sheets and the bottom of baking pans. It keeps cookies from sticking to the pans.

Pastry bag and tips: Pastry bags are helpful to pipe soft cookie dough and icing. If you do not have a pastry bag, a heavy-duty ziplock plastic bag with a small opening cut in one corner of the bag makes a fine substitute.

Pastry cutter: A pastry cutter is used to cut butter or shortening into flour. It usually has four or five parallel blades that curve into a handle on both ends, creating a "D" shape.

Rolling pin: A wooden rolling pin with ball-bearing handles is the ideal choice for rolling cookie dough.

Sifter: A sifter is an essential baking tool. It is used to combine dry ingredients by passing them through a fine-mesh screen. The rotating whisk inside the sifter breaks up any lumps and helps to create a uniform mixture.

Spatulas: Three types of spatulas are helpful for cookie making. A rubber spatula is used for scraping bowls and mixing blades, and is also used to fold in ingredients. An offset (L-shaped) spatula is used to move cutout cookies from the prep area to the cookie sheet. Wider, square-blade spatulas are useful in removing cookies from parchment or pans.

Tins: Cookie tins are useful to store baked cookies. They are airtight containers and come in assorted shapes and sizes. They also make ideal containers to package cookies for gift-giving.

Wax paper: Wax paper is different from parchment paper or plastic wrap. Wax paper is moisture-proof and nonstick, due to its wax coating. It is strongly recommended for wrapping cookie dough during the chilling process, for rolling cookie dough, and for layering cookies in storage tins.

Whisks: Wire whisks, specifically balloon whisks, are helpful for combining dry ingredients or lightly beating eggs. If you do not have a whisk, use a fork instead.

Wire cooling racks: Wire cooling racks are used to cool cookies. Most have a small-grid pattern. They come in a variety of sizes. Smaller racks are good for cooling baking pans. Larger racks can hold an entire sheet of cookies.

Zester: A zester is a small stainless steel tool with sharp, small holes at the end to shred citrus rind.

Master Recipes

ROYAL ICING

Royal icing is a classic powdered sugar icing that can be used in its natural white state, or colored with gluten-free food coloring. It is very versatile. You can use it to pipe a design, or you can simply spread the icing on a cookie. If you want to get fancy, you can layer colored sugars on top of the icing for a more elaborate design.

Two recipes are provided below. One uses meringue powder and the other uses egg whites. Both recipes yield the same result. If you have any concerns about using raw egg, use the meringue powder version. Meringue powder is gluten-free, consisting of dried egg whites, cornstarch, sugar, and a gum, such as cellulose or arabic. It can be found at some online merchants, in the craft /cake decorating aisle of some discount retailers such as Wal-Mart, or at specialty baking supply shops.

Royal Icing Using Meringue Powder

> 2 tablespoons meringue powder
>
> 3 tablespoons warm water
>
> 2⅔ cups powdered sugar

In the large bowl of an electric mixer, combine meringue powder and water. Set mixer speed to medium and beat until combined. Reduce speed to low and gradually add powdered sugar until completely blended. Set mixer speed to high and beat until thick and smooth, about 5 minutes. If mixture is too thick, add a little more water, a teaspoon at a time.

Royal Icing Using Egg Whites

> 2 large egg whites
>
> ⅛ teaspoon cream of tartar
>
> 2⅔ cups powdered sugar

In the large bowl of an electric mixer, combine egg whites and cream of tartar. Set mixer speed to medium. Beat until foamy. Reduce mixer speed to low and gradually add powdered sugar. Beat until blended. Set mixer speed to high and beat until thick and glossy, about 2 minutes.

Techniques for Decorating

Allow cookies to cool completely before decorating.

Divide icing into different bowls and color with gluten-free food coloring, if desired. Use a pastry bag, fitted with a narrow tip, to outline edges of the cookie or to pipe a decorative pattern. Lines, swirls, or ball designs are the easiest to make. Some basic and fancy techniques can be found online at: http://www.bakedecoratecelebrate.com/techniques.cfm?cat=9

If desired, outline the cookie or pipe a pattern. While the icing is still wet, use a small spoon to sprinkle the icing with sugar. Immediately invert the cookie to let the excess sugar fall off.

Let the icing set 1 to 2 hours, or overnight, to dry completely. Store any extra icing in an airtight container.

TOASTING NUTS

Toasting nuts adds a deeper, more complex nut flavor to cookies. It is easy to do.

Preheat oven to 350°F. Place nuts in a shallow baking pan. Bake 5 to 7 minutes until fragrant, stirring once or twice. If a recipe calls for lightly toasted nuts, bake nuts for no more than 5 minutes. Cool to room temperature, and then chop as instructed in recipe.

Metric Conversion Charts

TABLESPOONS AND OUNCES	GRAMS
(U.S. Customary System)	*(U.S. Customary System)*
1 pinch = less than ⅛ teaspoon (dry)	0.5 grams
1 dash = 3 drops to ¼ teaspoon (liquid)	1.25 grams
1 teaspoon (liquid)	5.0 grams
3 teaspoons = 1 tablespoon = ½ ounce	14.3 grams
2 tablespoons = 1 ounce	28.35 grams
4 tablespoons = 2 ounces = ¼ cup	56.7 grams
8 tablespoons = 4 ounces = ½ cup (1 stick of butter)	113.4 grams
8 tablespoons (flour) = about 2 ounces	72.0 grams
16 tablespoons = 8 ounces = 1 cup = ½ pound	226.8 grams
32 tablespoons = 16 ounces = 2 cups = 1 pound	453.6 grams
64 tablespoons = 32 ounces = 1 quart = 2 pounds	907.0 grams
1 quart = (roughly 1 liter)	

OVEN TEMPERATURE:

Fahrenheit	Celsius
300	148.8
325	162.8
350	177 (baking)
375	190.5
400	204.4 (hot oven)
425	218.3
450	232 (very hot oven)
475	246.1
500	260 (broiling)

CONVERSION FACTORS

ounces to grams: multiply ounce figure by 28.3 to get number of grams

grams to ounces: multiply gram figure by 0.0353 to get number of ounces

pounds to grams: multiply pound figure by 453.59 to get number of grams

pounds to kilograms: multiply pound figure by 0.45 to get number of kilograms

ounces to milliliters: multiply ounce figure by 30 to get numbers of milliliters

cups to liters: multiply cup figure by 0.24 to get number of liters

Fahrenheit to Celsius: subtract 32 from the Fahrenheit figure, multiply by 5, then divide by 9 to get Celsius figure

Celsius to Fahrenheit: multiply Celsius figure by 9, divide by 5, then add 32 to get Fahrenheit figure

Classics Revisited

No cookie book would be complete without a chapter on classic cookies. Here is a collection of irresistible chocolate chip, flourless peanut butter, buttery shortbread, and other cookies that will become your new gluten-free "classics."

Chocolate Chip and Pecan Cookies

Flourless Peanut Butter Cookies

Vanilla Bean Cookies

Shortbread Galettes

Ginger Molasses Cookies

Almond Lemon Biscotti

Old-Fashioned Sugar Cookies

Oatmeal Almond Cookies with Dates

Chocolate Chip and Pecan Cookies

MAKES 36 TO 42 COOKIES

Bittersweet chocolate chips (60% cocoa) make these a sophisticated treat for adults. Semisweet chips are a good alternative and result in a slightly sweeter taste. Whichever you choose, everyone will love these perfect chocolate chip cookies.

⅔ cup brown rice flour

3 tablespoons potato starch

1 tablespoon plus 2 teaspoons tapioca flour

½ teaspoon baking powder

½ teaspoon baking soda

¼ teaspoon xanthan gum

¼ teaspoon fine grain sea salt

¼ cup almond flour

4 tablespoons (½ stick) unsalted butter, room temperature

4 tablespoons vegetable shortening

½ cup packed dark brown sugar

¼ cup granulated sugar

1 teaspoon pure vanilla extract

1 large egg

2 cups (about 12 ounces) bittersweet or semisweet chocolate chips

1 cup chopped pecans

In a medium bowl, sift together brown rice flour, potato starch, tapioca flour, baking powder, baking soda, xanthan gum, and sea salt. Whisk in almond flour. Set aside.

In the large bowl of an electric mixer, combine butter, vegetable shortening, sugars, and vanilla extract. Set mixer speed to high and beat until fluffy, about 2 to 3 minutes. Add egg and beat for another 1 to 2 minutes. Reduce mixer speed to low and add flour mixture until just incorporated. Mix in the chocolate chips and pecans. Chill in a covered bowl for 1 to 2 hours, or overnight.

Preheat oven to 350°F. Line cookie sheets with parchment.

Using a medium cookie scoop, drop rounded tablespoons of dough onto prepared cookie sheets, spacing them about 2 inches apart. Bake until golden brown, about 12 to 15 minutes. Cool on cookie sheets for 2 minutes, and then transfer cookies, still on parchment, to wire racks to cool completely.

Store cookies in an airtight container for up to 1 week.

Flourless Peanut Butter Cookies

The delicious taste of peanut butter shines through in these unique flourless cookies. Mix the dough by hand for an easy one-bowl preparation. If you have peanut allergies, substitute unsalted, organic cashew butter and unsalted, roasted cashews for the peanut ingredients.

1 cup unsalted, creamy, organic
   peanut butter, room temperature

¾ cup granulated sugar

½ teaspoon baking soda

¼ teaspoon fine grain sea salt

1 large egg, lightly beaten

½ cup chopped unsalted, roasted
   peanuts

fine grain sea salt, to finish cookies
   (optional)

Preheat oven to 350°F. Line cookie sheets with parchment.

If oil has separated from the peanut butter, stir until all oil is mixed in and peanut butter has a smooth consistency.

In a large bowl, whisk together sugar, baking soda, and sea salt. Add peanut butter and beaten egg and stir with a large spoon until combined. Stir in chopped peanuts. The dough will be crumbly.

Using a medium cookie scoop, drop 1½-inch balls on prepared sheets, spacing them 2 inches apart. With the bottom of a glass or back of a spoon, flatten the balls to ½-inch thickness.

Bake for 12 to 15 minutes, until golden brown. Lightly sprinkle with fine grain sea salt, if desired. Cool completely on cookie sheets.

Store cookies in an airtight container for up to 1 week.

Baker's Note: Cashew butter is sometimes less moist than peanut butter. If you substitute cashew butter, you may want to add ¼ teaspoon vegetable oil prior to mixing.

Vanilla Bean Cookies

MAKES 60 TO 72 COOKIES

These light and crunchy vanilla bean cookies were the very first gluten-free cookies I created. I developed them for a friend's two sons, who have celiac disease. These cookies are made with vanilla sugar, an ingredient often found in Scandinavian or Eastern European cookies. They were inspired by a traditional Brazilian cookie that my girlfriend Paola makes. For a special treat, add mini chocolate chips.

1 cup granulated sugar

1 vanilla bean, cut into quarters

2 cups cornstarch

½ teaspoon fine grain sea salt

16 tablespoons (2 sticks) cold unsalted butter, cut into small pieces

½ teaspoon pure vanilla extract

1 large egg, lightly beaten

1 cup mini chocolate chips (optional)

Preheat oven to 375°F. Line cookie sheets with parchment.

In a food processor, pulse sugar and vanilla bean quarters until vanilla bean is pulverized. Sieve mixture to remove any seeds.

In a medium bowl, sift together vanilla sugar, cornstarch, and sea salt. Add butter. With a pastry cutter, cut in butter until dough resembles coarse meal. Mix in the vanilla extract and egg, combining thoroughly. Add chocolate chips, if desired. Chill for 30 to 40 minutes.

Using a small cookie scoop, shape the dough into ½-inch or ¾-inch balls, and drop onto prepared cookie sheets, spacing them about 2½ inches apart.

Bake for 8 to 10 minutes, until edges are golden brown. Cool on cookie sheets for 1 minute, and then transfer cookies, still on parchment, to wire racks to cool completely.

Store cookies in an airtight container for up to 1 week.

Baker's Note: You can buy premade vanilla sugar in gourmet food stores or from online merchants. Be sure that it is gluten-free.

Shortbread Galettes

I like to think of these delicate cookies as butter held together with a little sugar and flour. They are pure heaven and among the easiest to make.

⅔ cup brown rice flour

3 tablespoons potato starch

1 tablespoon plus 2 teaspoons tapioca flour

⅛ teaspoon fine grain sea salt

¼ teaspoon xanthan gum

¼ cup plus 2 tablespoons powdered sugar

¼ cup almond flour

8 tablespoons (1 stick) cold unsalted butter, cut into small pieces

granulated sugar, for sprinkling (optional)

In a medium bowl, sift brown rice flour, potato starch, tapioca flour, sea salt, xanthan gum, and powdered sugar. Whisk in almond flour. Add butter to flour mixture. With a pastry cutter, cut in butter until dough resembles coarse meal. Knead dough with hands until gathered and pliable. Wrap in plastic wrap or wax paper. Chill for 1 to 2 hours, or overnight.

Preheat oven to 350°F. Line cookie sheets with parchment.

Roll dough, between sheets of wax paper, to ⅓-inch thickness. Cut with 1-inch round cookie or biscuit cutter, dipping cookie cutter in brown rice flour or all-purpose gluten-free flour to aid cutting. Place cookies on prepared cookie sheets, spacing them about 2 inches apart. Leave cookies plain or sprinkle with granulated sugar. Bake until edges are golden brown, about 10 to 12 minutes. Cool on cookie sheets for 5 minutes. Transfer cookies, still on parchment, to wire racks to cool completely.

Store cookies in an airtight container for up to 5 days.

Baker's Note: If dough has been chilled overnight, let it stand for 2 to 3 minutes, prior to rolling, so that it is pliable.

Ginger Molasses Cookies

MAKES 36 TO 42 COOKIES

These tender cookies are the greatest milk dunkers ever! Their melt-in-your-mouth texture and big flavor will please everyone in your family. Be sure to use fresh orange zest, to bring out the best in these old-fashioned standbys.

1⅓ cups brown rice flour

⅓ cup plus 1½ tablespoons potato starch

3 tablespoons plus 1 teaspoon tapioca flour

2 teaspoons baking soda

½ teaspoon xanthan gum

2 teaspoons ground ginger

1½ teaspoons ground cinnamon

1 teaspoon ground cloves

1 teaspoon salt

½ cup almond flour

4 tablespoons (½ stick) unsalted butter, room temperature

8 tablespoons vegetable shortening

1 cup packed dark brown sugar

1 large egg

¼ cup molasses

2 teaspoons grated orange zest

granulated sugar, for rolling

In a medium bowl, sift together brown rice flour, potato starch, tapioca flour, baking soda, xanthan gum, spices, and salt. Whisk in almond flour. Set aside.

In the large bowl of an electric mixer, combine butter, vegetable shortening, and brown sugar. Set mixer speed to high and beat until fluffy, 2 to 3 minutes. Add egg, molasses, and orange zest, and beat another 1 to 2 minutes. Reduce mixer speed to low, add flour mixture, and mix until just incorporated. Chill in a covered bowl, for 1 to 2 hours, or overnight.

Preheat oven to 350°F. Line cookie sheets with parchment.

Using a medium cookie scoop, shape the dough into 1½-inch balls. Roll balls in granulated sugar and arrange on prepared sheets, spacing them about 2½ to 3 inches apart. Bake until golden brown and cracked on top, about 12 to 15 minutes. Cool on cookie sheets for 5 minutes. Transfer cookies, still on parchment, to wire racks to cool completely.

Store in airtight container for up to 1 week.

Almond Lemon Biscotti

MAKES 36 TO 42 COOKIES

There is nothing quite like crunchy biscotti. These cookies are great as a snack or served as an after-dinner accompaniment to a glass of wine or a dish of ice cream or fruit.

1 cup brown rice flour

⅓ cup potato starch

2½ tablespoons tapioca flour

½ teaspoon baking powder

½ teaspoon baking soda

½ teaspoon xanthan gum

¼ teaspoon salt

½ cup plus 2 tablespoons almond flour

8 tablespoons (1 stick) unsalted butter, room temperature

1 cup granulated sugar, plus extra for sprinkling

2 teaspoons grated lemon zest

1 teaspoon pure vanilla extract

1 teaspoon pure almond extract

2 large eggs

1 cup coarsely chopped toasted whole almonds

In a medium bowl, sift together brown rice flour, potato starch, tapioca flour, baking powder, baking soda, xanthan gum, and salt. Whisk in almond flour. Set aside.

In the large bowl of an electric mixer, combine butter and 1 cup sugar. Set mixer speed to high and beat until fluffy, 2 to 3 minutes. Add lemon zest, vanilla extract, and almond extract. Mix until thoroughly combined. Add eggs, one at a time, and beat until light and fluffy, about 2 minutes. Reduce mixer speed to low and add flour mixture until just incorporated. Mix in the chopped almonds. Chill in a covered bowl, for 1 to 2 hours, or overnight.

Preheat oven to 350°F. Line cookie sheet with parchment.

Divide the dough in half. Place one half on a sheet of wax paper and roll into a log 2½ to 3 inches in diameter and about 9 inches long. Repeat with the other half of dough. Place both logs on a single cookie sheet, spacing well apart. Generously sprinkle the tops with sugar. Bake until firm to touch, about 30 to 35 minutes. Cool on cookie sheet for 15 minutes.

Carefully transfer the logs to a work area. With a serrated knife, cut logs crosswise into slices about ½ inch thick.

Lay the slices flat on cool, parchment-lined cookie sheets. Bake until golden brown, about 10 to 12 minutes. Transfer cookies, still on parchment, to wire racks to cool completely.

Store cookies in an airtight container for up to 2 weeks.

Old-Fashioned Sugar Cookies

MAKES 48 TO 60 COOKIES

I developed this recipe for my friend Gail. She was diagnosed with celiac disease late in life, and really missed her sweets. She told me that these cookies reminded her of the sugar cookies her grandmother made.

1 cup brown rice flour

⅓ cup potato starch

2½ tablespoons tapioca flour

½ teaspoon xanthan gum

½ teaspoon baking soda

½ teaspoon cream of tartar

⅛ teaspoon salt

¼ cup plus 2 tablespoons almond flour

8 tablespoons (1 stick) unsalted butter, room temperature

¾ cup sugar

1 teaspoon pure vanilla extract

1 large egg

granulated, demerara, or gluten-free sanding sugar, for sprinkling

In a medium bowl, sift together brown rice flour, potato starch, tapioca flour, xanthan gum, baking soda, cream of tartar, and salt. Whisk in almond flour. Set aside.

In the large bowl of an electric mixer, combine butter and sugar. Set mixer speed to medium and beat until light and fluffy. Add vanilla extract and egg. Beat until well combined, about 1 to 2 minutes. Reduce mixer speed to low. Add flour mixture and mix until just incorporated. Divide dough into quarters, and wrap each quarter in plastic wrap or wax paper. Chill for 1 to 2 hours, or overnight.

Preheat oven to 350°F. Line cookie sheets with parchment.

Roll dough, one quarter at a time, between sheets of wax paper, to ¼-inch thickness. Cut with 1-inch round cookie cutter, dipping cookie cutter in brown rice flour or all-purpose gluten-free flour to aid cutting. Place cookies on prepared cookie sheets, spacing them about 2 inches apart. If dough becomes too soft to reroll easily, return it to the refrigerator or place it in the freezer for 5 to 10 minutes, until it is firm enough to reroll.

Sprinkle cookies with granulated sugar, demerara sugar, or gluten-free sanding sugar. Bake until edges are pale golden brown, about 10 to 12 minutes. Cool on cookie sheets for 5 minutes. Transfer cookies, still on parchment, to wire racks to cool completely.

Store cookies in an airtight container for up to 1 week.

Oatmeal Almond Cookies with Dates

MAKES 30 TO 36 COOKIES

I developed these sweet, chewy oatmeal cookies for my brother Ken. He asked me to make an oatmeal cookie for him that was lighter in texture than ordinary oatmeal cookies and sweetened with dates. I originally made these cookies with almonds, but I like them with walnuts, too.

⅓ cup brown rice flour

1½ tablespoons potato starch

2½ teaspoons tapioca flour

½ teaspoon baking soda

¼ teaspoon baking powder

¼ teaspoon xanthan gum

⅛ teaspoon salt

2 tablespoons almond flour

8 tablespoons (1 stick) unsalted butter, room temperature

½ cup packed dark brown sugar

½ cup granulated sugar

1 teaspoon pure vanilla extract

1 large egg

1½ cups gluten-free rolled oats

½ cup coarsely chopped whole almonds

½ cup coarsely chopped dates

In a medium bowl, sift together brown rice flour, potato starch, tapioca flour, baking soda, baking powder, xanthan gum, and salt. Whisk in almond flour. Set aside.

In the large bowl of an electric mixer, combine butter, sugars, and vanilla extract. Set mixer speed to high and beat until fluffy, about 2 to 3 minutes. Add egg and beat another 1 to 2 minutes. Reduce mixer speed to low and add flour mixture and oats, alternating, until just incorporated. Mix in the almonds and dates. Chill in a covered bowl for at least 2 hours, or overnight.

Preheat oven to 375°F. Line cookie sheets with parchment.

Using a small cookie scoop, drop rounded tablespoons onto prepared sheets, spacing them about 2½ inches apart. Bake until light brown, about 10 to 12 minutes. Cool on cookie sheets for 2 minutes. Transfer cookies, still on parchment, to wire racks to cool completely.

Store cookies in an airtight container for up to 1 week.

Baker's Note: Don't crowd cookies on the cookie sheet, as they have a tendency to spread. Use a #40 scoop if you want a larger cookie.

Especially for Children

A freshly baked cookie, warm out of the oven, is everyone's favorite treat. Try the "Pizza Cookie" for a birthday party, or make the Jam Thumbprints or Chocolate Peanut Butter Cups as a special after-school treat. You will find that these fun cookies appeal to the kid in each of us.

Jam Thumbprints

Decorated Cookie Cutouts

Double-Chocolate "Pizza Cookie"

Sweet Cinnamon Snickerdoodles

No-Bake Chocolate Oatmeal Drops

Gingerbread Cookies

Matt's No-Bake Chocolate Cherry Crispies

Chocolate Peanut Butter Cups

Jam Thumbprints

MAKES 42 TO 48 COOKIES

Over the years, I have experimented with a dozen Jam Thumbprint recipe variations. This version has a buttery flavor, light texture, and tender crumb that contrast nicely with its jam filling. I like it best with slightly tangy jams like sour cherry, raspberry, or apricot.

1 cup plus 2½ tablespoons brown rice flour

⅓ cup plus 2¼ teaspoons potato starch

3 tablespoons plus ¾ teaspoon tapioca flour

½ teaspoon xanthan gum

½ teaspoon baking powder

½ teaspoon fine grain sea salt

¼ cup plus 3 tablespoons almond flour

12 tablespoons (1½ sticks) unsalted butter, room temperature

⅔ cup sugar

1 large egg

1 teaspoon pure vanilla extract

¼ cup sour cherry, apricot, or raspberry jam

In a medium bowl, sift brown rice flour, potato starch, tapioca flour, xanthan gum, baking powder, and sea salt. Whisk in almond flour. Set aside.

In the large bowl of an electric mixer, combine butter and sugar. Set mixer speed to high and beat until fluffy, about 3 to 4 minutes. Add egg and vanilla extract and beat until just combined. Reduce mixer speed to low. Add flour mixture and mix until just incorporated. Chill in a covered bowl, for 1 to 2 hours, or overnight.

Preheat oven to 350°F. Line cookie sheets with parchment.

Using a small cookie scoop, drop 1-inch balls onto prepared cookie sheets, spacing them about 2 inches apart. Press a thumbprint about ½ inch deep into the center of each cookie. Fill each indentation with ¼ teaspoon jam. Bake until the edges of the cookies are golden brown, about 12 to 14 minutes. Cool completely on cookie sheets placed on wire racks.

Store cookies in an airtight container for up to 5 days.

Baker's Note: I use a small wooden honey dipper to make the "thumb" indentation.

Decorated Cookie Cutouts

Create childhood memories with these buttery cutout cookies. For best results, use 1-inch cookie cutters in simple shapes. Decorate with colored sanding sugars before baking, or use Royal Icing to pipe interesting designs onto baked cookies. Let your imagination be your guide.

⅔ cup brown rice flour

3 tablespoons potato starch

1 tablespoon plus 2 teaspoons tapioca flour

½ teaspoon xanthan gum

¼ cup almond flour

8 tablespoons (1 stick) unsalted butter, room temperature

¼ cup sugar

1 teaspoon pure vanilla extract

1 large egg

granulated sugar, gluten-free sanding sugar, or gluten-free sprinkles, for sprinkling unbaked cookies (optional)

Royal Icing (see page 24) or powdered sugar, for icing baked cookies (optional)

In a medium bowl, sift together brown rice flour, potato starch, tapioca flour, and xanthan gum. Whisk in almond flour. Set aside.

In the large bowl of an electric mixer, combine butter and sugar. Set mixer speed to medium and beat until light and fluffy, about 1 to 2 minutes. Add vanilla extract and egg. Beat 2 to 3 minutes more until well combined. Reduce mixer speed to low. Add flour mixture and mix until just incorporated. Divide dough into quarters, and wrap each quarter in plastic wrap or wax paper. Chill for 1 to 2 hours, or overnight.

Preheat oven to 350°F. Line cookie sheets with parchment.

Roll dough, one quarter at a time, between sheets of wax paper, to ¼-inch thickness. Cut with cookie cutter, dipping cookie cutter in brown rice flour or all-purpose gluten-free flour to aid cutting. Place cookies on prepared cookie sheets, spacing them about 2 inches apart. If dough becomes too soft to reroll easily, return it to the refrigerator or place it in the freezer for 5 to 10 minutes, until it is firm enough to reroll.

Before baking, sprinkle cookies with granulated sugar, gluten-free sanding sugar, or gluten-free sprinkles. Alternatively, bake cookies plain, and after cooling, decorate with icing or sprinkle with powdered sugar. Bake until edges are golden brown, about 10 to 12 minutes. Cool on cookie sheets for 5 minutes. Transfer cookies, still on parchment, to wire racks to cool completely.

Store cookies in an airtight container for up to 1 week.

Double-Chocolate "Pizza Cookie"

MAKES ONE 12-INCH OR TWO 9-INCH COOKIES

This "yummy-in-the-tummy," giant-size double-chocolate cookie makes a fun surprise for a child's party or special celebration. The dough is firm enough so that the kids can help bake as well as decorate. Make either as one giant 12-inch cookie, or layer two 9-inch cookies together with icing, and frost the top, to look like a cake.

1 cup brown rice flour

⅓ cup potato starch

2½ tablespoons tapioca flour

½ teaspoon xanthan gum

½ teaspoon baking soda

¼ teaspoon salt

¼ cup Dutch-process cocoa

¼ cup plus 2 tablespoons almond flour

10 tablespoons (1¼ sticks) unsalted butter, room temperature

½ cup packed light brown sugar

¼ cup granulated sugar

1 teaspoon pure vanilla extract

1 large egg

2 cups mini chocolate chips

TOPPING:

¾ cup semisweet or bittersweet chocolate chips

6 tablespoons (¾ stick) unsalted butter, room temperature

1½ cups powdered sugar

¾ cup cream cheese, room temperature

½ cup mini M&M candies (optional)

1½ tablespoons gluten-free sprinkles (optional)

¼ cup gluten-free mini marshmallows (optional)

In a medium bowl, sift together brown rice flour, potato starch, tapioca flour, xanthan gum, baking soda, salt, and cocoa. Whisk in almond flour. Set aside.

In the large bowl of an electric mixer, combine butter and sugars. Set mixer speed to high and beat until light and fluffy, about 2 to 3 minutes. Add vanilla extract and egg. Beat until light and fluffy, about 1 to 2 more minutes. Reduce speed to low. Add flour mixture and mix until just incorporated. Stir in the chocolate chips. Chill in a covered bowl, for 1 to 2 hours, or overnight.

Preheat oven to 350°F. Line one round 12-inch diameter baking or pizza pan, or two 9-inch diameter baking or springform pans, with parchment. Lightly butter parchment and dust with all-purpose gluten-free flour. If using 9-inch diameter baking pans, they should be no more than 2 inches deep for easy cookie removal.

Press the chilled cookie dough evenly into the prepared pan. It should have a uniform thickness of about ¼ inch. Bake until firm to touch, about 20 to 25 minutes.

Remove cookie from the oven and cool completely in the pan. Gently remove the cookie from the pan and transfer it to a wire rack.

For the topping: In a double boiler, set over simmering water, melt chocolate chips. Cool to room temperature.

In the large bowl of an electric mixer, combine butter and powdered sugar. Set mixer speed to high and beat until thoroughly combined. Add cream cheese and melted chocolate. Beat until thoroughly combined. Spread icing on cooled cookie. Decorate with mini M&M candies, gluten-free sprinkles, or mini marshmallows.

Baker's Note: Wilton Industries' online store sells giant 12-inch cookie pans as well as 9-inch springform pans.

Sweet Cinnamon Snickerdoodles

MAKES 24 TO 36 COOKIES

Light, buttery snickerdoodles were the very first cookies I ever made. They were standard fare in my 4-H baking class. Although my tastes have broadened since those days, I still love the sweet, spicy cinnamon flavor of these old favorites.

⅔ cup plus 2½ tablespoons brown rice flour

3 tablespoons plus 2¼ teaspoons potato starch

2 tablespoons plus ¼ teaspoon tapioca flour

1 teaspoon cream of tartar

½ teaspoon baking soda

¼ teaspoon xanthan gum

¼ teaspoon salt

1 teaspoon ground cinnamon, plus 1 teaspoon extra for topping

¼ cup plus 1 tablespoon almond flour

8 tablespoons (1 stick) unsalted butter, room temperature

¾ cup granulated sugar, plus 2 tablespoons extra for topping

1 large egg

In a medium bowl, sift together brown rice flour, potato starch, tapioca flour, cream of tartar, baking soda, xanthan gum, salt, and 1 teaspoon cinnamon. Whisk in almond flour. Set aside.

In the large bowl of an electric mixer, combine butter and ¾ cup sugar. Set mixer speed to high and beat until fluffy, about 2 to 3 minutes. Add egg and beat another 1 to 2 minutes. Reduce mixer speed to low. Add flour mixture and mix until incorporated. Chill in a covered bowl for 1 to 2 hours, or overnight.

Preheat oven to 400°F. Line cookie sheets with parchment.

In a small bowl, combine remaining 2 tablespoons sugar and 1 teaspoon cinnamon. Using a small cookie scoop, shape the dough into 1-inch balls and roll them in the cinnamon-sugar topping. Place cookies on prepared cookie sheets, spacing them about 3 inches apart. Bake until cookies begin to crack, about 10 to 12 minutes. Cool on cookie sheets for 5 minutes. Transfer cookies, still on parchment, to wire racks to cool completely.

Store cookies in an airtight container for up to 1 week.

No-Bake Chocolate Oatmeal Drops

These cookies have a rich, fudgy texture. They are great slipped into lunch boxes or backpacks. Use bittersweet chocolate if you prefer cookies that are not too sweet.

4 tablespoons (½ stick) unsalted butter, room temperature

¼ cup whole milk

1 cup granulated sugar

½ cup semisweet or bittersweet (60% cocoa) chocolate chips

½ teaspoon pure vanilla extract

1½ cups gluten-free rolled oats

½ cup chopped walnuts

Line cookie sheets with parchment.

In a saucepan, combine the butter, milk, and sugar. Bring to a rolling boil, and then boil for exactly 1 minute. Stir in chocolate chips until melted. Add vanilla extract, oats, and walnuts. Stir until thoroughly combined. Remove from heat.

Using a medium cookie scoop, drop rounded tablespoons of dough onto prepared cookie sheets. Refrigerate until set, about 20 minutes.

Store at room temperature, in an airtight container, for up to 1 week.

Baker's Note: Do not boil sugar mixture more than 1 minute, or the cookie dough may not stick together.

Gingerbread Cookies

This recipe makes melt-in-your-mouth gingerbread cookies. Use 1½- to 2-inch cookie cutters to make gingerbread boys and girls or an entire menagerie, and then decorate with Royal Icing and raisins or candies.

1⅓ cups brown rice flour

⅓ cup plus 1½ tablespoons potato starch

3 tablespoons plus 1 teaspoon tapioca flour

½ teaspoon baking soda

½ teaspoon xanthan gum

1 teaspoon ground ginger

1 teaspoon ground cloves

½ teaspoon ground cinnamon

½ teaspoon ground nutmeg

½ teaspoon salt

½ cup almond flour

8 tablespoons (1 stick) unsalted butter, room temperature

¼ cup packed light brown sugar

½ cup molasses

2 tablespoons heavy cream

Royal Icing (see page 24)

½ cup currants, raisins, mini M&Ms, or other gluten-free candies, for decoration

In a medium bowl, sift together brown rice flour, potato starch, tapioca flour, baking soda, xanthan gum, spices, and salt. Whisk in almond flour. Set aside.

In the large bowl of an electric mixer, with speed set to high, cream butter. Add brown sugar and molasses and beat until light and fluffy, about 2 to 3 minutes. Reduce mixer speed to low. Add flour mixture and mix until incorporated. Add cream and mix until just incorporated. Divide dough into eight pieces, and wrap each piece in plastic wrap or wax paper. Chill for at least 3 hours, or overnight.

Preheat oven to 350°F. Line cookie sheets with parchment.

Roll dough, one piece at a time, between sheets of wax paper, to ¼-inch thickness. Cut with 1½-inch or 2-inch cookie cutters, dipping cookie cutter in brown rice flour or all-purpose gluten-free flour to aid cutting. Place cookies on prepared cookie sheets, spacing them about 2½ inches apart. If dough becomes too soft to reroll easily, return it to the refrigerator or place it in the freezer for 5 to 10 minutes, until it is firm enough to reroll.

Bake until firm to touch, about 10 to 12 minutes. Cool on cookie sheets for 2 minutes, and then transfer cookies, still on parchment, to wire racks to cool completely. Decorate with Royal Icing and currants, raisins, or candies when completely cool.

Store cookies in an airtight container for up to 1 week, layered between sheets of parchment or wax paper.

Matt's No-Bake Chocolate Cherry Crispies

MAKES 18 TO 24 COOKIES

When I started planning my cookbook recipes, my friend Matt asked me to include the no-bake, crispy-rice cookies of his childhood. My answer was, "Well, no — something like them, but more sophisticated."

8 ounces bittersweet chocolate, chopped (use only high-quality, gluten-free chocolate)

2 tablespoons (¼ stick) unsalted butter, room temperature

2 cups gluten-free crisp rice cereal

½ cup dried cherries, coarsely chopped

Line cookie sheets with parchment.

In a double boiler, set over simmering water, melt chocolate and butter. Stir in rice cereal and dried cherries. Mix until thoroughly combined. Remove from heat.

Using a medium cookie scoop, drop rounded tablespoons of dough onto prepared cookie sheets. Refrigerate until set, about 20 minutes.

Store cookies in an airtight container for up to 1 week.

Baker's Note: For a sweeter cookie, replace the bittersweet chocolate with semi-sweet chocolate.

Chocolate Peanut Butter Cups

MAKES 48 TO 60 COOKIES

My niece, Annie, loves this adaptation of thumbprint cookies. These cookies taste like peanut-butter-cup candies, and they disappear fast. For those with peanut allergies, organic almond butter can be substituted for peanut butter. Delicious for all ages!

1 cup plus 2½ tablespoons brown rice flour

⅓ cup plus 2¼ teaspoons potato starch

2 tablespoons plus 2¾ teaspoons tapioca flour

1 teaspoon baking soda

½ teaspoon baking powder

½ teaspoon xanthan gum

½ teaspoon salt

⅔ cup Dutch-process cocoa

¼ cup plus 3 tablespoons almond flour

6 tablespoons (¾ stick) unsalted butter, room temperature

½ cup vegetable shortening

1 cup granulated sugar, plus extra for rolling

1 large egg

1 teaspoon pure vanilla extract

FILLING:

¾ cup creamy, unsalted, organic peanut butter

3 tablespoons (⅜ stick) unsalted butter, room temperature

¾ teaspoon pure vanilla extract

1 large egg white

½ cup powdered sugar

In a medium bowl, sift together brown rice flour, potato starch, tapioca flour, baking soda, baking powder, xanthan gum, salt, and cocoa. Whisk in almond flour. Set aside.

In the large bowl of an electric mixer, combine butter, vegetable shortening, and 1 cup sugar. Set speed to high and beat until fluffy, about 2 to 3 minutes. Add egg and vanilla extract. Beat until light and fluffy, about 2 to 3 minutes. Reduce mixer speed to low. Add flour mixture, mixing until just incorporated. Chill in a covered bowl, for 1 to 2 hours, or overnight.

Preheat oven to 350°F. Line cookie sheets with parchment.

Mix filling just before baking cookies.

For the filling: In the small bowl of an electric mixer, combine peanut butter, butter, and vanilla extract. Set mixer speed to medium and beat until smooth. Add egg white and beat until well incorporated. Reduce mixer speed to low and mix in the powdered sugar. Set aside.

Using a small cookie scoop, form the base cookie dough into 1-inch balls. Roll the balls in granulated sugar. Place balls on prepared cookie sheets, spacing about 2 inches apart. Make an indentation, about ¼ inch deep, in the center of each ball.

Shape a level ½ teaspoon of the peanut butter filling into a small ball, and place it in the indentation of each cookie. Gently push the edges of the indentation over the peanut butter ball until only the top of the ball is visible.

Bake cookies until puffed and slightly cracked on top, about 10 to 12 minutes. Cool on cookie sheets for 1 to 2 minutes. Transfer cookies, still on parchment, to wire racks to cool completely.

Store cookies in an airtight container for up to 3 days.

Baker's Note: Any leftover peanut butter filling can be baked into flourless peanut butter treats. Roll leftover filling into 1½-inch balls, and bake until golden brown, about 10 to 12 minutes. Cool on cookie sheets for 2 minutes. Transfer cookies, still on parchment, to wire racks to cool completely.

Fruit Delights

Nothing beats a bite of fruit locked in an ethereal embrace with sugar. These fruit-infused, flavor-packed treats will be loved by everyone.

Banana Bites

Apricot and Polenta Jewels

Lemon Drops

Date Walnut Logs

Cranberry-Orange-Nut Drops

Coconut Surprises

Krissy's Apple Cookies

Frosted Pumpkin Currant Cookies

Blueberry Jam Sandwiches

Banana Bites

These light and chewy banana cookies are a healthy option for everyone, including gluten-tolerant folks. Easy to make, they rely on the banana and dates, instead of sugar, for the sweetener.

1½ ripe bananas

½ cup finely chopped pitted dates

2 tablespoons flaked, sweetened coconut, chopped

¾ cup plus 2 tablespoons gluten-free rolled oats

2½ tablespoons extra-light olive oil

½ teaspoon pure vanilla extract

Preheat oven to 350°F. Line cookie sheets with parchment.

In a medium bowl, mash the bananas. Add remaining ingredients and thoroughly mix. Let stand at room temperature for 15 minutes.

Using a small cookie scoop, drop teaspoonfuls of dough onto prepared cookie sheets. Flatten slightly with the back of a spoon or bottom of a glass. Bake until golden brown, about 20 minutes. Cool completely on cookie sheets placed on wire racks.

Store cookies in an airtight container for up to 2 days.

Baker's Note: These cookies have a short shelf life and are best when eaten within 1 or 2 days.

Apricot and Polenta Jewels

MAKES 48 TO 60 COOKIES

Frequently I experiment with some new ingredients or a new concept. Cornmeal and apricots proved to be the perfect combination for these crunchy, not-too-sweet cookies, which are a delicious change of pace when you want to explore something new. I love them plain, but you can also roll them in sugar or sprinkle the tops with sugar before baking.

⅔ cup brown rice flour plus additional ½ teaspoon for tossing apricots

3 tablespoons potato starch

1 tablespoon plus 2 teaspoons tapioca flour

½ teaspoon baking soda

¼ teaspoon xanthan gum

¼ teaspoon fine grain sea salt

¼ cup almond flour

⅓ cup finely ground yellow cornmeal

½ cup granulated sugar, plus ¼ cup granulated sugar for rolling or sprinkling (optional)

⅓ cup chopped dried apricots

8 tablespoons (1 stick) cold unsalted butter, cut into small pieces

1 large egg, lightly beaten

½ teaspoon pure vanilla extract

½ teaspoon pure almond extract

In a medium bowl, sift together ⅔ cup brown rice flour, potato starch, tapioca flour, baking soda, xanthan gum, and sea salt. Whisk in almond flour, cornmeal, and ½ cup sugar.

In a small bowl, toss chopped apricots in ½ teaspoon brown rice flour.

Add butter to bowl containing flour mixture. Using a pastry cutter, cut butter into flour mixture until it resembles coarse crumbs. Stir in chopped apricots (discard any flour that did not stick to the apricots). Add egg, vanilla extract, and almond extract. Mix dough until gathered and pliable. Apricots should be evenly distributed throughout the dough. Divide dough in half. Roll each half into a log 1½ inches in diameter and about 9 inches long. Wrap in plastic wrap or wax paper. Chill for 1 to 2 hours, or overnight.

Preheat oven to 350°F. Line cookie sheets with parchment.

If rolling in sugar, sprinkle ¼ cup sugar on parchment or wax paper. Unwrap each log and roll it in the sugar until thoroughly coated.

Cut log (sugared or plain) into ¼-inch-thick slices, and place slices about 2 inches apart on prepared cookie sheets. Sprinkle with granulated sugar, if desired. Bake until pale golden brown, about 10 to 12 minutes. Cool on cookie sheets for 2 minutes. Transfer cookies, still on parchment, to wire racks to cool completely.

Store cookies in an airtight container for up to 1 week.

Baker's Note: Slide the wrapped cookie log inside an empty cardboard paper towel roll, before chilling, to help it keep its cylindrical shape.

Lemon Drops

These melt-in-your-mouth lemon drops remind me of freshly squeezed lemonade. Their big lemon taste comes from lemon juice, lemon zest, and lemon oil. I use Boyajian lemon oil, which can be found at gourmet markets or from online merchants. If you cannot find lemon oil, substitute lemon extract and extra lemon zest.

1 cup brown rice flour

⅓ cup potato starch

2½ tablespoons tapioca flour

¼ teaspoon xanthan gum

½ cup cornstarch

¼ cup plus 2 tablespoons almond flour

16 tablespoons (2 sticks) unsalted butter, room temperature

½ cup powdered sugar, plus extra for dusting cookies

2 tablespoons fresh lemon juice

1 teaspoon grated lemon zest

½ teaspoon lemon oil (or substitute 1 teaspoon lemon extract plus 1 additional teaspoon grated lemon zest)

In a medium bowl, sift together brown rice flour, potato starch, tapioca flour, xanthan gum, and cornstarch. Whisk in almond flour. Set aside.

In the large bowl of an electric mixer, combine butter and ½ cup powdered sugar. Set mixer speed to high and beat until light and fluffy, about 1 to 2 minutes. Add lemon juice, lemon zest, and lemon oil. Beat until combined, about 1 more minute. Add flour mixture and beat until smooth. Chill in a covered bowl, for 1 to 2 hours, or overnight.

Preheat oven to 350°F. Line cookie sheets with parchment.

Using a small cookie scoop, shape dough into 1-inch balls. Place them on prepared cookie sheets, spacing them about 1 inch apart. Bake until pale golden on top and lightly browned on the bottom, about 15 to 18 minutes. Immediately sift a generous amount of powdered sugar over cookies. Cool completely on cookie sheets placed on wire racks. Dust with more powdered sugar before serving.

Store cookies in an airtight container for up to 1 week, layered between sheets of parchment or wax paper.

Baker's Note: For a fun variation, substitute orange juice, orange zest, and orange oil for the lemon equivalents.

Date Walnut Logs

MAKES 30 TO 36 COOKIES

Whenever a friend asks for an easy-to-bake, gluten-free cookie, this is the recipe I share. The fruit creates a dense, moist cookie, great for special occasions or a special treat for a lunch box.

1 cup ground walnuts

½ cup ground pitted dates

¾ cup flaked, sweetened coconut, chopped

½ cup packed dark brown sugar

1 large egg, lightly beaten

¼ cup flaked, sweetened coconut, chopped, for rolling

¼ cup chopped walnuts, for rolling

Preheat oven to 350°F. Lightly grease cookie sheets.

In a large bowl, mix ground walnuts, dates, chopped coconut, brown sugar, and egg until thoroughly combined. Mixture will be a sticky paste.

In a small bowl, mix together ¼ cup chopped coconut and ¼ cup chopped walnuts for topping.

Using 2 teaspoons of dough, shape a small log, about ¾ inch in diameter and 1¼ inches long. Roll log in coconut and walnut topping. Place on greased cookie sheet. Repeat with remaining dough and topping, and place logs about 2 inches apart on cookie sheets.

Bake until golden brown, about 12 minutes. Transfer to wire racks and cool completely.

Store cookies in an airtight container for up to 1 week.

Baker's Note: Keep a bowl of water handy to clean sticky fingers.

Cranberry-Orange-Nut Drops

MAKES 30 TO 36 COOKIES

These moist, soft cookies are loaded with tangy cranberries, orange zest, pistachios, and walnuts, a delightfully refreshing combination. These cookies are wonderful any time of the year and make a colorful addition to a holiday cookie platter.

1¼ cup dried sweetened cranberries, chopped

2½ tablespoons orange juice

⅔ cup brown rice flour

3 tablespoons potato starch

1 tablespoon plus 2 teaspoons tapioca flour

½ teaspoon baking powder

¼ teaspoon xanthan gum

⅛ teaspoon baking soda

⅛ teaspoon salt

½ teaspoon ground cinnamon

¼ teaspoon ground ginger

¼ cup almond flour

8 tablespoons (1 stick) unsalted butter, room temperature

½ cup packed light brown sugar

1 large egg

2 teaspoons grated orange zest

1 teaspoon pure vanilla extract

½ cup chopped walnuts

½ cup chopped unsalted, shelled, natural pistachios

In a small bowl, combine dried cranberries and orange juice. Let stand 30 to 40 minutes, until cranberries soften and juice is absorbed. Stir occasionally.

In a medium bowl, sift together brown rice flour, potato starch, tapioca flour, baking powder, xanthan gum, baking soda, salt, and spices. Whisk in almond flour. Set aside.

In the large bowl of an electric mixer, combine butter and brown sugar. Set mixer speed to high and beat until smooth. Add egg, orange zest, and vanilla extract. Beat until well blended, about 2 minutes. Reduce mixer speed to low. Add flour mixture and mix until incorporated. Mix in the walnuts, pistachios, and cranberries, along with any accumulated juices. Chill in a covered bowl, for 1 to 2 hours, or overnight.

Preheat oven to 350°F. Line cookie sheets with parchment.

Using a medium cookie scoop, drop rounded tablespoons of dough onto prepared cookie sheets, spacing them about 2 inches apart. Bake until golden, about 15 to 18 minutes. Cool on cookie sheets for 5 minutes. Transfer cookies, still on parchment, to wire racks to cool completely.

Store cookies in an airtight container for up to 5 days, layered between sheets of parchment or wax paper.

Coconut Surprises

A bittersweet chocolate chip is the tasty surprise in the center of these easy, moist, coconut macaroons.

1 cup flaked, sweetened coconut, finely chopped

½ cup flaked, unsweetened coconut, finely chopped

⅓ cup sugar

⅛ teaspoon salt

½ teaspoon pure vanilla extract

½ teaspoon pure almond extract

1 large egg white, lightly beaten

1 teaspoon water

12 to 18 bittersweet (60% cocoa) chocolate chips

powdered sugar, for dusting (optional)

Preheat oven to 350°F. Line cookie sheets with parchment.

In a medium bowl, whisk together coconuts, sugar, and salt. Using a large spoon, mix in vanilla and almond extracts. Add egg white and water. Mix well until mixture is moistened and starts to hold together.

Roll 2 teaspoons of coconut mixture into a ball. Make an indentation in the center of each ball and insert a chocolate chip. Reroll the ball to conceal the chocolate chip.

Arrange balls 1 inch apart on prepared cookie sheets. Bake until bottoms are golden and balls are puffed but still white, about 12 to 15 minutes.

Transfer cookies, still on parchment, to wire racks to cool completely. If desired, dust lightly with powdered sugar before serving.

Store cookies in an airtight container for up to 5 days.

Baker's Note: This is a sticky dough, so keep a bowl of water handy to clean your fingers as you work.

Krissy's Apple Cookies

MAKES 30 TO 36 COOKIES

My friend Krissy has lupus and is allergic to almost everything. When I made these tangy, sweet apple cookies for her, she gave me a huge hug.

1 large Granny Smith apple

1 cup unsalted whole almonds

½ cup flaked, unsweetened coconut

¼ cup chopped dried apricots

2 teaspoons extra-light or
extra-virgin olive oil

2 tablespoons honey or agave nectar

1 teaspoon pure vanilla extract

1 large egg, lightly beaten

Preheat oven to 350°F. Line cookie sheets with parchment.

Peel and quarter apple. Remove seeds and core. Cut into 1-inch chunks, about 24 to 36 pieces.

In the large bowl of a food processor, combine apple chunks with all ingredients, except egg. Pulse until coarsely ground. Add egg. Pulse 3 or 4 times to mix in.

Using a small cookie scoop, shape dough into 1-inch balls. Drop onto prepared cookie sheets, spacing them 2 inches apart. With the bottom of a glass, flatten balls to ¼-inch thickness. Wipe glass frequently to keep it clean.

Bake until light brown and firm to touch, about 15 to 20 minutes. Cool cookies on cookie sheets for 5 minutes. Transfer cookies, still on parchment, to wire racks to cool completely.

Store cookies in airtight container for up to 2 days.

Baker's Note: These cookies are best when eaten within 1 or 2 days. Please note that foods containing honey should not be fed to children less than one year of age because their digestive systems cannot process the spores which are naturally found in honey.

Frosted Pumpkin Currant Spice Cookies

MAKES 36 TO 48 COOKIES

These soft, cakelike spice cookies are great made with either fresh or canned pumpkin. The browned-butter frosting lends a celebratory feeling. I like them best with dried zante currants, but chopped raisins or dried cranberries work well, too.

⅔ cup brown rice flour

3 tablespoons potato starch

1 tablespoon plus 2 teaspoons tapioca flour

¼ teaspoon baking powder

¼ teaspoon baking soda

¼ teaspoon xanthan gum

¼ teaspoon salt

¼ teaspoon ground cinnamon

¼ teaspoon ground cloves

¼ teaspoon ground ginger

¼ teaspoon ground nutmeg

¼ cup almond flour

½ cup dried zante currants

½ cup chopped walnuts

4 tablespoons (½ stick) unsalted butter, room temperature

¼ cup packed dark brown sugar

¼ cup honey

1 large egg

½ cup canned or fresh pumpkin puree

BROWNED BUTTER FROSTING:

2 tablespoons (¼ stick) unsalted butter, room temperature

1½ cups powdered sugar

3 to 4 tablespoons heavy cream

In a medium bowl, sift together brown rice flour, potato starch, tapioca flour, baking powder, baking soda, xanthan gum, salt, and spices. Whisk in almond flour. Set aside.

In a small bowl, toss currants and walnuts together.

In the large bowl of an electric mixer, with the speed set to medium, cream the butter. Add brown sugar and honey. Beat until fluffy, about 2 to 3 minutes. Add egg and beat another 1 to 2 minutes. Add pumpkin puree and mix until thoroughly combined. Reduce mixer speed to low. Add flour mixture and mix until just incorporated. Mix in the currants and walnuts. Chill in a covered bowl, for 1 to 2 hours, or overnight.

Preheat oven to 375°F. Line cookie sheets with parchment.

Using a small cookie scoop, drop rounded teaspoons of dough onto prepared cookie sheets, spacing them about 2 inches apart. Bake until golden brown, about 15 to 18 minutes. Cool on cookie sheets for 2 minutes. Transfer cookies, still on parchment, to wire racks. Cool for 5 more minutes. Frost while cookies are still warm.

For Browned Butter Frosting: In a small saucepan, melt butter and heat until it foams. Reduce heat to low and cook until the foam along the edges begins to turn golden, about 3 to 5 minutes. Remove from heat and stir in powdered sugar. Add cream slowly, until proper consistency for spreading is attained.

One at a time, invert each cookie, dip top in icing, and swirl. Place cookie on wire rack until icing dries and cookie is completely cool.

Store cookies in an airtight container for up to 1 week, layered between sheets of parchment or wax paper.

Baker's Note: Zante currants are dried, seedless black grapes that are smaller and more tart than raisins.

Blueberry Jam Sandwiches

Be prepared for lots of praise when you make these cookies. The blueberry jam is an ideal match for the lemon-hazelnut cookie base. If you want a less sweet treat, these buttery lemon cookies are also excellent served without the jam.

⅔ cup brown rice flour

3 tablespoons potato starch

1 tablespoon plus 2 teaspoons tapioca flour

¼ teaspoon xanthan gum

¼ cup almond flour

2 tablespoons finely ground toasted hazelnuts

8 tablespoons (1 stick) unsalted butter, room temperature

½ cup granulated sugar, plus extra sugar for sprinkling (optional)

1 tablespoon grated lemon zest

⅛ teaspoon fine grain sea salt

1 large egg yolk

½ cup good-quality blueberry jam

In a medium bowl, sift together brown rice flour, potato starch, tapioca flour, and xanthan gum. Whisk in almond flour and finely ground hazelnuts. Set aside.

In the large bowl of an electric mixer, combine the butter, sugar, lemon zest, and salt. Set mixer speed to high and beat until light and fluffy, about 2 minutes. Add egg yolk and beat until blended. Reduce mixer speed to low. Add flour mixture and mix until just incorporated. Gather dough together and divide in half. Wrap each half in wax paper or plastic wrap. Chill for at least 6 hours.

Preheat oven to 400°F. Line cookie sheets with parchment.

Roll dough, one half at a time, between sheets of wax paper, to ¼-inch thickness. Cut with 1-inch round cookie cutter, dipping cookie cutter in brown rice flour or all-purpose gluten-free flour to aid cutting. Place cookies on prepared cookie sheets, spacing them about 2 inches apart. If dough becomes too soft to reroll easily, return it to the refrigerator or place it in the freezer for 5 to 10 minutes, until it is firm enough to reroll.

If desired, sprinkle half of the unbaked cookies with sugar. Bake until edges are pale golden brown, about 8 to 10 minutes. Cool on cookie sheets for 3 minutes. Transfer cookies, still on the parchment, to wire racks to cool completely.

Just before serving, spread 1 teaspoon of jam over flat side of each unsugared cookie, then place one sugared cookie on top, with sugared side up. Serve filled cookies immediately.

Unfilled cookies can be stored in an airtight container for up to 5 days.

Baker's Note: For best results, use a gourmet wild blueberry jam.

Bars and Squares

Brownies and other bar cookies are so easy to make,
and they evoke the best memories of childhood and family fun.
Make these for a special dessert or an afternoon treat.

Double-Chocolate Brownies with Walnuts

Macadamia Nut Blondies

Rocky Road S'Mores Bars

Lemon Squares

Chocolate Orange Bars with Hazelnuts

Fruit and Nut Granola Bars

Double-Cherry Streusel Bars

Chocolate Raspberry Fingers

Double-Chocolate Brownies with Walnuts

MAKES 16 COOKIES

These moist brownies are extra chocolaty because of the chocolate chips that are added to the batter.

½ cup brown rice flour

2½ tablespoons potato starch

1 tablespoon plus ¾ teaspoon tapioca flour

½ teaspoon xanthan gum

3 tablespoons almond flour

3 ounces unsweetened chocolate

8 tablespoons (1 stick) unsalted butter, room temperature

3 large eggs

1¼ cups granulated sugar

½ teaspoon salt

1 teaspoon pure vanilla extract

½ cup coarsely chopped walnuts

¾ cup semisweet chocolate chips

Preheat oven to 350°F. Line the sides and bottom of an 8 x 8-inch baking pan with aluminum foil, leaving an overhang of about 2-inches on each of two opposite edges. Cut a piece of parchment paper to fit the bottom of the pan. Place parchment on top of foil.

In a medium bowl, sift together brown rice flour, potato starch, tapioca flour, and xanthan gum. Whisk in almond flour. Set aside.

In the top of a double boiler, set over simmering water, melt unsweetened chocolate and butter. Stir constantly, until chocolate and butter are fully combined and mixture is smooth. Remove from heat and let cool to room temperature.

In the large bowl of an electric mixer, combine eggs, sugar, salt, and vanilla extract. Set mixer speed to high and beat until mixture thickens and becomes pale in color, about 1 to 2 minutes. Turn off mixer. Using a rubber spatula, fold chocolate mixture into egg mixture. Take care not to deflate the batter. Fold in flour mixture in two portions. Carefully fold in walnuts and chocolate chips.

Pour batter into prepared baking pan. Smooth top. Bake until top is slightly cracked and just firm to touch, about 35 to 40 minutes. Cool uncut cookies in baking pan on a wire rack. Lift uncut cookies out of pan, using foil overhang as an aid, and cut into 16 cookies.

Store cookies in an airtight container, at room temperature, for up to 3 days, or refrigerate for a longer shelf life.

Baker's Note: Pecans or toasted hazelnuts can be substituted for walnuts.

Macadamia Nut Blondies

MAKES 16 COOKIES

According to food historians, blondies and brownies originated at the beginning of the twentieth century. These blondies, made with macadamia nuts and white chocolate, are truly a classic. I use Ghirardelli's white chocolate baking bar for this recipe, as it is gluten-free.

⅔ cup brown rice flour

3 tablespoons potato starch

1 tablespoon plus 2 teaspoons tapioca flour

½ teaspoon xanthan gum

¼ teaspoon salt

¼ cup almond flour

8 tablespoons (1 stick) unsalted butter, room temperature

1½ cups packed light brown sugar

1 teaspoon pure vanilla extract

2 large eggs

¾ cup coarsely chopped macadamia nuts

3 ounces white chocolate, coarsely chopped

Preheat oven to 350°F. Line the sides and bottom of an 8 x 8-inch baking pan with aluminum foil, leaving an overhang of about 2-inches on each of two opposite edges. Cut a piece of parchment paper to fit the bottom of the pan. Place parchment on top of foil. Lightly butter parchment and foil-covered sides of pan.

In a medium bowl, sift together brown rice flour, potato starch, tapioca flour, xanthan gum, and salt. Whisk in almond flour. Set aside.

In the large bowl of an electric mixer, combine butter, brown sugar, and vanilla extract. Set mixer speed to high and beat until fluffy, about 2 to 3 minutes. Add eggs and beat until incorporated, about 1 to 2 minutes. Reduce mixer speed to low and add flour mixture until just incorporated. Mix in chopped macadamia nuts and white chocolate.

Spoon batter into prepared baking pan. Smooth top. Bake until top is slightly cracked and firm to touch in the center, about 40 to 45 minutes. Cool uncut cookies in baking pan on a wire rack. Lift uncut cookies out of pan, using foil overhang as an aid, and cut into 16 cookies.

Store cookies in an airtight container, at room temperature, for up to 3 days, or refrigerate for longer shelf life.

Baker's Note: Ghirardelli classic white chocolate chips are not gluten-free, but their white chocolate baking bar is.

Rocky Road S'Mores Bars

MAKES 20 COOKIES

My youngest niece, Kaili, loves chocolate and marshmallow treats of all kinds. This combination of a rocky road bar and s'mores treat is her favorite. This cookie is great for a family movie night or a rainy-day campout in the living room. Be sure to use gluten-free graham crackers and gluten-free marshmallows.

½ cup brown rice flour

2½ tablespoons potato starch

1 tablespoon plus ¾ teaspoon tapioca flour

¼ teaspoon xanthan gum

3 tablespoons almond flour

¾ cup gluten-free graham cracker crumbs (about 6 crushed graham crackers)

½ cup packed light brown sugar

8 tablespoons (1 stick) cold unsalted butter, cut into small pieces

1 large egg, lightly beaten

TOPPING:

¾ cup semisweet chocolate chips

¾ cup milk chocolate chips

2 tablespoons heavy cream

1 cup gluten-free miniature marshmallows

½ cup coarsely chopped walnuts

Preheat oven to 350°F. Line the sides and bottom of a 13 x 9-inch or 12 x 8-inch baking pan with aluminum foil, leaving an overhang of about 2-inches on each of two opposite edges.

In a medium bowl, sift together brown rice flour, potato starch, tapioca flour, and xanthan gum. Whisk in almond flour.

In the large bowl of a food processor, combine flour mixture, graham cracker crumbs, and brown sugar. Pulse to mix. Add butter, pulsing until mixture resembles coarse meal. Add egg, pulsing until just combined.

Press dough evenly into the bottom of prepared baking pan and smooth top. Bake until firm to touch, about 20 to 25 minutes. While crust is baking, prepare topping.

For the topping: Coarsely chop ¼ cup of the semisweet chocolate chips and ¼ cup of the milk chocolate chips. In a saucepan over low heat, heat cream until simmering. Add chopped chocolate chips, stirring until completely melted. Remove from heat. Set aside.

As soon as crust comes out of the oven, sprinkle remaining chocolate chips, marshmallows, and walnuts evenly over crust, and press down lightly with fingers. Drizzle melted chocolate over the top and return baking pan to oven. Bake until marshmallows puff and begin to turn golden, about 7 to 8 minutes. Cool uncut cookies in baking pan on a wire rack. If necessary, refrigerate until topping is firm, about 1 to 2 hours. Lift uncut cookies out of pan, using foil overhang as an aid, and cut into 20 cookies.

Store cookies in an airtight container for up to 5 days.

Baker's Note: For a sweeter cookie, replace the semisweet chocolate chips with ¾ cup milk chocolate chips.

Lemon Squares

These tangy lemon cookies have just the right amount of gusto to satisfy a lemon craving. Prepare the filling while the crust is baking, so that it can go back into the oven immediately.

⅔ cup brown rice flour

3 tablespoons potato starch

1 tablespoon plus 2 teaspoons tapioca flour

¼ teaspoon xanthan gum

⅛ teaspoon salt

¼ cup almond flour

¼ cup granulated sugar

8 tablespoons (1 stick) cold unsalted butter, cut into small pieces

FILLING:

2 large eggs

¾ cup granulated sugar

¼ cup fresh lemon juice

1 teaspoon grated lemon zest

1 tablespoon plus 1 teaspoon brown rice flour

1⅛ teaspoon potato starch

¾ teaspoon cornstarch

¼ teaspoon baking powder

TOPPING:

½ cup powdered sugar, sifted

Line the sides and bottom of an 8 x 8-inch baking pan with aluminum foil, leaving an overhang of about 2-inches on each of two opposite edges. Cut a piece of parchment paper to fit the bottom of the pan. Place parchment on top of foil.

In a medium bowl, sift together brown rice flour, potato starch, tapioca flour, xanthan gum, and salt. Whisk in almond flour and sugar. Add butter. Using a pastry cutter, cut butter into flour-sugar mixture until it resembles coarse crumbs. Press dough evenly into the bottom of prepared baking pan. Refrigerate for about 30 minutes.

Preheat oven to 350°F. Bake crust until edges are light brown and center is golden brown, about 30 to 40 minutes. While crust is baking, prepare filling.

For the filling: In the large bowl of an electric mixer, combine eggs and sugar. Set mixer speed to high, and beat until mixture is light and fluffy, about 2 to 3 minutes. Add lemon juice and lemon zest. Beat until combined. Add brown rice flour, potato starch, cornstarch, and baking powder. Beat until well combined.

Gently pour filling over hot crust. Smooth top and return baking pan to oven. Bake until filling sets, about 20 to 25 minutes. Remove from oven and immediately sprinkle with about half of the powdered sugar. Cool uncut cookies in baking pan on a wire rack. When cool, sprinkle with remaining powdered sugar. Lift uncut cookies out of pan, using foil overhang as an aid, and cut into 16 cookies.

Store cookies in an airtight container, at room temperature, for up to 3 days, or refrigerate for longer shelf life.

Chocolate Orange Bars with Hazelnuts

Chocolate, orange, and hazelnuts make these bar cookies an elegant treat. They are moist, tender, and flavorful.

½ cup brown rice flour

2½ tablespoons potato starch

1 tablespoon plus ¾ teaspoon tapioca flour

1 teaspoon baking powder

½ teaspoon xanthan gum

3 tablespoons almond flour

3 tablespoons finely ground toasted hazelnuts

3 ounces unsweetened chocolate

6 tablespoons (¾ stick) unsalted butter, room temperature

2 large eggs

½ cup packed light brown sugar

1 teaspoon pure vanilla extract

1 tablespoon grated orange zest

pinch salt

½ cup orange juice

½ cup coarsely chopped toasted hazelnuts

Preheat oven to 350°F. Line the sides and bottom of an 8 x 8-inch baking pan with aluminum foil, leaving an overhang of about 2-inches on each of two opposite edges. Lightly butter foil-covered bottom and sides of pan. Dust with gluten-free all-purpose flour. Shake out any excess flour.

In a medium bowl, sift together brown rice flour, potato starch, tapioca flour, baking powder, and xanthan gum. Whisk in almond flour and finely ground hazelnuts. Set aside.

In the top of a double boiler, set over simmering water, melt unsweetened chocolate and butter. Stir constantly, until chocolate and butter are fully combined and mixture is smooth. Remove from heat and let cool to room temperature.

In the large bowl of an electric mixer, with mixer speed set to high, beat eggs until foamy. Add brown sugar, vanilla extract, orange zest, and salt. Beat until thoroughly incorporated, about 1 to 2 minutes. Reduce mixer speed to low. Add chocolate mixture and mix until combined. Add orange juice and mix until combined. Add flour mixture and mix until just incorporated. Mix in chopped hazelnuts.

Spoon batter into prepared baking pan. Smooth top. Bake until top is springy to touch and pulling away from the sides of the pan, about 30 to 35 minutes. Cool uncut cookies completely in baking pan on a wire rack. Lift uncut cookies out of pan, using foil overhang as an aid, and cut into 16 cookies.

Store cookies in an airtight container, at room temperature, for up to 3 days, or refrigerate for longer shelf life.

Fruit and Nut Granola Bars

MAKES 16 COOKIES

These granola bars are an easy treat to make. Take them along on your next hike in the woods or on your daily journey to school or work. Walnuts or pecans can be substituted for the almonds. Be sure to use rolled oats that are processed in a gluten-free environment.

8 tablespoons (1 stick) unsalted butter, room temperature

¼ cup packed dark brown sugar

½ cup pure maple syrup

¼ cup light corn syrup

½ teaspoon salt

½ teaspoon pure vanilla extract or ¼ teaspoon gluten-free pure maple extract

2 cups gluten-free rolled oats

½ cup coarsely chopped whole almonds

¼ cup unsalted shelled sunflower seeds

¼ cup unsalted shelled pumpkin seeds (pepitas)

¼ cup chopped dried apricots

¼ cup dried cranberries, chopped

¼ cup flaked, sweetened coconut, chopped

Preheat oven to 400°F. Line the sides and bottom of a 13 x 9-inch or 12 x 8-inch baking pan with aluminum foil, leaving an overhang of about 2-inches on each of two opposite edges. Cut parchment to fit the bottom of the pan. Lightly oil parchment and foil-covered sides of pan.

In a medium saucepan, combine butter, brown sugar, syrups, and salt over low heat. Stir constantly until butter and sugar are melted. Bring mixture to a full boil. Boil for just over 1 minute. Immediately remove from heat. Stir in vanilla or maple extract. Stir in all the remaining ingredients. Mix well, until liquid is thoroughly incorporated.

Pour mixture into prepared baking pan and press into an even layer.

Bake until deep golden brown and bubbly, about 18 to 20 minutes. Cool uncut cookies in baking pan on wire rack. After 20 minutes, while still warm, score the bars for cutting, but do not cut through. Cool completely. Lift uncut cookies out of pan, using foil overhang as an aid, and cut into 16 cookies.

Store cookies in an airtight container for up to 1 week.

Double-Cherry Streusel Bars

MAKES 24 COOKIES

I don't know what I like more, the sweet-tart cherry filling or the almond and coconut streusel topping. It's hard to resist these moist, tasty bars. They are great as a simple dessert or an indulgent snack.

1⅓ cups brown rice flour

⅓ cup plus 1½ tablespoons potato starch

3 tablespoons plus 1 teaspoon tapioca flour

½ teaspoon xanthan gum

¼ teaspoon ground cinnamon

¼ teaspoon salt

½ cup almond flour

⅔ cup granulated sugar

12 tablespoons (1½ sticks) cold unsalted butter, cut into small pieces

1½ teaspoons pure vanilla extract

½ teaspoon pure almond extract

FILLING:

1 cup dried sweet cherries (about 6 ounces)

1 cup tart cherry preserves (about 12 ounces)

1 tablespoon fresh lemon juice

1 tablespoon granulated sugar

TOPPING:

¾ cup flaked, sweetened coconut

½ cup sliced almonds

Preheat oven to 375°F. Line the sides and bottom of a 13 x 9-inch or 12 x 8-inch baking pan with aluminum foil, leaving an overhang of about 2-inches on each of two opposite edges.

In a medium bowl, sift together brown rice flour, potato starch, tapioca flour, xanthan gum, cinnamon, and salt. Whisk in almond flour and sugar.

In the large bowl of a food processor, combine flour-sugar mixture, butter, vanilla extract, and almond extract. Pulse until mixture resembles coarse meal. Transfer ¾ cup of mixture to medium-sized bowl and set aside for topping. Blend remaining mixture in processor until large clumps form.

Press dough evenly into the bottom of prepared baking pan. Pierce entire surface of dough with a fork. Bake until golden, about 20 to 22 minutes. Remove from oven and cool for 15 minutes before adding the filling and streusel topping.

For the filling: In the large bowl of a food processor, combine dried cherries, cherry preserves, lemon juice, and sugar. Blend into a chunky puree.

For the topping: Add coconut and almonds to the bowl containing the reserved dough. Mix with a fork, breaking into small clumps.

After crust has cooled for 15 minutes, spread cherry filling evenly over crust. Sprinkle topping evenly over filling and pat down lightly. Return baking pan to oven and bake until topping is golden brown, about 25 to 30 minutes. Cool uncut cookies completely in baking pan on a wire rack. Lift uncut cookies out of pan, using foil overhang as an aid, and cut into 24 cookies.

Chocolate Raspberry Fingers

MAKES 20 COOKIES

Chocolate raspberry fingers are my absolute favorite bar cookie. The thin chocolate crust, tangy raspberry-chocolate filling, and light almond-egg white topping are flavorful and slightly gooey, making it the ideal comfort bar. Prepare the filling while the crust is baking, so that it can go back into the oven immediately.

⅓ cup brown rice flour

1½ tablespoons potato starch

2½ teaspoons tapioca flour

¼ teaspoon xanthan gum

⅛ teaspoon fine sea salt

1½ tablespoons unsweetened cocoa (not Dutch-process)

2 tablespoons almond flour

4 tablespoons (½ stick) unsalted butter, room temperature

¼ cup granulated sugar

½ teaspoon pure vanilla extract

FILLING:

⅔ cup almond flour

2 large egg whites

½ cup granulated sugar

½ teaspoon pure almond extract

¼ cup plus 2 tablespoons seedless raspberry jam, stirred until smooth

½ cup semisweet chocolate chips

2 tablespoons finely chopped blanched almonds

Preheat oven to 350°F. Line the sides and bottom of an 8 x 8-inch baking pan with aluminum foil, leaving an overhang of about 2-inches on each of two opposite edges.

In a medium bowl, sift together brown rice flour, potato starch, tapioca flour, xanthan gum, sea salt, and cocoa. Whisk in almond flour. Set aside.

In the large bowl of an electric mixer, combine butter, sugar, and vanilla extract. Set mixer speed to high and beat until light and fluffy, about 1 to 2 minutes. Reduce mixer speed to low. Add flour mixture and mix until combined. Dough will be crumbly. Press dough evenly into the bottom of prepared pan. Pierce entire surface of dough with a fork. Bake until firm to touch, about 20 to 25 minutes. While crust is baking, prepare filling.

For the filling: In the large bowl of a food processor, pulse almond flour, egg whites, sugar, and almond extract until well blended. Set aside.

As soon as crust comes out of the oven, spread raspberry jam evenly over crust. Sprinkle with chocolate chips. Pour almond-egg white mixture evenly over crust. Sprinkle with finely chopped almonds. Press almonds down lightly. Return pan to oven and bake until topping is puffy and golden, about 20 to 25 minutes. Cool uncut cookies completely in baking pan on a wire rack. Lift uncut cookies out of pan, using foil overhang as an aid, and cut into 20 cookies.

Store cookies in an airtight container for up to 3 days.

Meringues Only

There is nothing like a light, sweet meringue that dissolves
when it hits your tongue. These meringue recipes offer a variety
of flavorful sensations, including nutty brown sugar, raspberry-chocolate,
lavender, and fig-date-walnut. They pay homage to this classic
cookie that originated in the late seventeenth century.

Brown Sugar Pecan Kisses

Fudge-Filled Drops

Chocolate Chip Raspberry Meringues

Hazelnut Meringues

Double-Berry Meringues

Lavender Clouds

Fruit and Nut Bonbons

Chocolate Almond Dreams

Brown Sugar Pecan Kisses

MAKES 24 TO 36 COOKIES

Brown sugar and toasted pecans give these nutty cookies a deeper, more complex flavor than ordinary meringues. They have a crispy exterior and a soft, chewy interior.

1 large egg white

pinch cream of tartar

pinch salt

¾ cup packed dark brown sugar

½ teaspoon pure vanilla extract

2 cups chopped toasted pecans

Preheat oven to 300°F. Line cookie sheets with parchment.

In the small bowl of an electric mixer, combine egg white, cream of tartar, and salt. Set mixer speed to high. Beat until soft peaks form. Add brown sugar, 1 tablespoon at a time, until stiff peaks form, about 3 to 5 minutes. Turn off mixer. Carefully fold in vanilla extract using a rubber spatula. Carefully fold in pecans, one third at a time, so as not to deflate the batter.

Using a small cookie scoop, drop rounded teaspoons of batter onto prepared cookie sheets, spacing them about 2 inches apart. Bake until firm to touch, about 20 to 25 minutes. Transfer cookies, still on parchment, to wire racks to cool completely.

Store cookies in an airtight container for up to 3 days.

Baker's Note: If using a glass bowl, rinse it in warm water and dry thoroughly before beating the egg. The warmth from the bowl will help the egg form peaks faster.

Fudge-Filled Drops

MAKES 24 TO 36 COOKIES

The pistachio-fudge filling gives these almond meringue cookies an intriguing texture and unique flavor. They are a terrific fancy dessert choice for special celebrations. If you don't have pistachios, sliced almonds can be substituted.

2 large egg whites

⅛ teaspoon cream of tartar

⅛ teaspoon salt

½ cup superfine sugar

¼ teaspoon pure almond extract

FILLING:

2 large egg yolks

2 tablespoons powdered sugar

4 tablespoons (½ stick) unsalted butter, room temperature

½ cup semisweet chocolate chips

2 tablespoons finely chopped unsalted natural pistachios

Preheat oven to 250°F. Line cookie sheets with parchment.

In the small bowl of an electric mixer, combine egg whites, cream of tartar, and salt. Set mixer speed to high. Beat until soft peaks form. Add sugar, 1 tablespoon at a time, until stiff peaks form, about 3 to 5 minutes. Set mixer speed to low and mix in almond extract.

Drop double teaspoons of batter onto prepared cookie sheets, spacing them about 2 inches apart. With the back of a spoon, make a ½-inch-deep depression in the center of each cookie, and push the edges higher to create a bird's-nest shape. Bake until firm to touch, about 35 to 40 minutes. Transfer cookies, still on parchment, to wire racks to cool completely.

For the filling: In a small bowl, beat egg yolks lightly and stir in powdered sugar.

In a small saucepan over low heat, melt butter and chocolate chips. Add egg mixture. Cook for 1 to 2 minutes, stirring constantly. Remove from heat and stir until cool.

Fill each meringue with a teaspoonful of the filling, and sprinkle with finely chopped pistachios.

Store cookies in an airtight container for up to 3 days.

Baker's Note: If cookies lose their depression while baking, use the handle of a spoon to gently tap a small well in the center for the filling.

Chocolate Chip Raspberry Meringues

MAKES 54 TO 60 COOKIES

Everyone loves the playful pink color of these flavor-packed meringues. They are made extra-special by the addition of miniature chocolate chips.

½ cup superfine sugar

2 tablespoons plus 1 teaspoon
   raspberry gelatin powder

2 large egg whites

pinch of salt

½ teaspoon white vinegar

⅔ cup mini chocolate chips

Preheat oven to 250°F. Line cookie sheets with parchment.

In a small bowl, whisk together sugar and gelatin.

In the small bowl of an electric mixer, combine egg whites and salt. Set mixer speed to high. Beat until foamy. Add sugar-gelatin mixture, 1 tablespoon at a time, until stiff peaks form and gelatin is completely dissolved, about 3 to 5 minutes. Set mixer speed to low and mix in vinegar. Turn off mixer and, using a rubber spatula, carefully fold in chocolate chips so as not to deflate the batter.

Drop double teaspoons of batter onto prepared cookie sheets, spacing them about 2 inches apart. Bake for 30 minutes. Turn oven off and leave cookies in oven for an additional 20 minutes. Transfer cookies, still on parchment, to wire racks to cool completely.

Store cookies in an airtight container for up to 3 days.

Hazelnut Meringues

Hazelnut meringues make a wonderful party treat. Their light texture and nutty flavor create a sophisticated cookie that everyone will appreciate. I love hazelnuts, but toasted pecans can be substituted.

½ cup superfine sugar

1 cup toasted hazelnuts

2 large egg whites

⅛ teaspoon salt

Preheat oven to 250°F. Line cookie sheets with parchment.

In the small bowl of a food processor, combine ¼ cup of the sugar and all the hazelnuts. Pulse until finely ground.

In the small bowl of an electric mixer, combine egg whites and salt. Set mixer speed to high. Beat until soft peaks form. Add remaining ¼ cup sugar, 1 tablespoon at a time, until stiff peaks form, about 3 to 5 minutes. Turn off mixer and, using a rubber spatula, carefully fold in sugar-hazelnut mixture so as not to deflate the batter.

Drop double teaspoons of batter onto prepared cookie sheets, spacing them about 2 inches apart. Flatten slightly with the back of a spoon. Bake until firm to touch, about 30 minutes. Transfer cookies, still on parchment, to wire racks to cool completely.

Store cookies in an airtight container for up to 5 days.

Double-Berry Meringues

Sweet, dried blueberries and cherries make these melt-in-your-mouth meringues perfect for a light afternoon snack. Their luscious fruity center will have everyone coming back for more.

½ cup superfine sugar

¼ cup powdered sugar

2 large egg whites

⅛ teaspoon salt

⅛ teaspoon cream of tartar

¼ cup dried blueberries, chopped

¼ cup dried cherries, chopped

Preheat oven to 250°F. Line cookie sheets with parchment.

In a small bowl, whisk together superfine sugar and powdered sugar.

In the small bowl of an electric mixer, combine egg whites, salt, and cream of tartar. Set mixer speed to high. Beat until soft peaks form. Add sugar mixture, 1 tablespoon at a time, until stiff peaks form, about 3 to 5 minutes. Turn off mixer. Using a rubber spatula, carefully fold in dried berries so as not to deflate the batter.

Drop rounded tablespoons of batter onto prepared cookie sheets, spacing them about 2 inches apart. Bake for 30 minutes. Turn oven off and leave cookies in oven for an additional 20 minutes. Transfer cookies, still on parchment, to wire racks to cool completely.

Store cookies in an airtight container for up to 3 days.

Baker's Note: If you prefer, use ½ cup of just one type of berry.

Lavender Clouds

MAKES 30 TO 36 COOKIES

Culinary-grade lavender buds lend a subtle floral and slightly tangy flavor to these unique meringues. You can find lavender buds in specialty herb or tea stores. For a spicy variation, pulse 2 teaspoons of finely chopped crystallized ginger with sugar and lavender buds until finely ground.

½ cup superfine sugar

¼ cup powdered sugar

1 tablespoon culinary-quality, dried lavender buds

2 large egg whites

⅛ teaspoon salt

⅛ teaspoon cream of tartar

¼ teaspoon pure vanilla extract

Preheat oven to 250°F. Line cookie sheets with parchment.

In the small bowl of a food processor, combine the superfine sugar, powdered sugar, and lavender. Pulse until lavender is finely ground.

In the small bowl of an electric mixer, with mixer set to high speed, beat egg whites until foamy. Add salt and cream of tartar. Beat until soft peaks form. Add the lavender-sugar mixture, 1 tablespoon at a time, and beat until stiff peaks form. Set mixer speed to low and mix in vanilla extract.

Drop double teaspoons of batter onto prepared cookie sheets, spacing them about 2 inches apart. Bake until firm to touch and tops are faintly cracked, about 30 to 35 minutes. Transfer cookies, still on parchment, to wire racks to cool completely.

Store cookies in an airtight container for up to 5 days.

Baker's Note: If you prefer, pipe batter onto cookie sheets using a pastry bag fitted with a ½-inch plain tip, or you can use a heavy-duty ziplock plastic bag with a very small opening cut in one corner of the bag.

Fruit and Nut Bonbons

The natural sweetness of the dates and dried figs makes this meringue a delicious confection. Use California Mission or Turkish figs, for the best results.

¼ cup ground or very finely chopped dates

¼ cup ground or very finely chopped dried figs

¼ cup ground walnuts

½ teaspoon pure vanilla extract

1 large egg white

pinch salt

⅓ cup superfine sugar

Preheat oven to 250°F. Line cookie sheets with parchment.

In a medium bowl, combine dates, figs, walnuts, and ¼ teaspoon vanilla extract. Mix thoroughly. The mixture will be sticky. Shape a level ½ teaspoon of the mixture into a ball. Arrange the balls on wax paper. Set aside.

In the small bowl of an electric mixer, combine egg white and salt. Set mixer speed to high. Beat until foamy. Add sugar, 1 tablespoon at a time, and beat until stiff peaks form. Reduce mixer speed to low and mix in remaining ¼ teaspoon vanilla extract.

Roll fruit-nut balls, one at a time, in egg-white mixture, coating completely. Place on prepared cookie sheets, spacing them about 2 inches apart. Bake until firm to touch, about 30 minutes. Transfer cookies, still on parchment, to wire racks to cool completely.

Store cookies in an airtight container for up to 3 days.

Baker's Note: If you cannot find dried figs, you can substitute an additional ¼ cup of dates.

Chocolate Almond Dreams

MAKES 36 TO 48 COOKIES

These cookies are light and chewy, like a macaroon. They are especially delicious with a dish of dark chocolate ice cream.

2 large egg whites

pinch cream of tartar

pinch salt

⅔ cup superfine sugar

⅛ teaspoon pure vanilla extract

1⅓ cups coarsely chopped toasted slivered, blanched almonds

2 ounces semisweet or bittersweet chocolate, finely chopped or grated

Preheat oven to 275°F. Line cookie sheets with parchment.

In the small bowl of an electric mixer, with mixer set to high speed, beat egg whites until foamy. Add cream of tartar and salt. Beat until soft peaks form. Add sugar 1 tablespoon at a time, and beat until stiff peaks form. Add vanilla extract and beat until combined. Turn off mixer and, using a rubber spatula, carefully fold in almonds and chocolate so as not to deflate the batter.

Drop double teaspoonfuls of batter onto prepared cookie sheets, spacing them about 2 inches apart. Flatten slightly with the back of a spoon. Bake until lightly browned and tops are beginning to crack, about 20 to 25 minutes. Cool cookies completely on cookie sheets placed on wire racks.

Store cookies in an airtight container for up to 5 days.

Celebrations and Sharing

Cookies are perfect for birthdays, holidays, family gatherings, or whenever people get together. Package these delicious homemade treats in a tin and give as a gift or share at a cookie swap.

French Chocolate Macaroons

Pecan Wedding Cakes

Chocolate Peppermint Cookies

Almond Hazelnut Cookies

Chocolate Orange Crunchies

Walnut Citrus Cookies

Five-Spice Ginger Cookies

Double-Chocolate and Double-Hazelnut Biscotti

Pine Nut Cookies

French Chocolate Macaroons

MAKES 24 TO 30 FILLED COOKIES

French macaroons are the ultimate in gluten-free cookies, made for centuries with ground almonds, sugar, and egg whites. Traditionally they are filled with a layer of ganache, jam, or flavored buttercream. These authentic macaroons (*les macarons*) are the dainty type found in the best bakeries in Paris. They are a bit tricky, but well worth the effort. The easy-to-make ganache filling, sandwiched between two cookie halves, gives them a deep, chocolaty flavor.

½ cup whole blanched almonds

2 tablespoons packed light brown sugar

1 cup powdered sugar

3 tablespoons Dutch-process cocoa

2 large egg whites

pinch cream of tartar

2 tablespoons superfine sugar

1 teaspoon pure vanilla extract

FILLING:

3 tablespoons heavy cream

2 ounces bittersweet chocolate, finely chopped

Preheat oven to 350°F. Line cookie sheets with parchment.

In the large bowl of a food processor, combine whole almonds, light brown sugar, and ⅔ cup of the powdered sugar. Pulse until almonds are pulverized. Add remaining powdered sugar and cocoa. Pulse until well mixed. Set aside.

In the small bowl of an electric mixer, combine egg whites and cream of tartar. Set mixer speed to high. Beat until soft peaks form. Gradually add the superfine sugar and beat until stiff peaks form, about 2 minutes. Set mixer speed to low and mix in vanilla extract. Turn off mixer and, using a rubber spatula, fold in almond mixture in two portions until combined, being careful not to deflate the batter.

Transfer batter to a pastry bag fitted with a ½-inch plain tip, or a heavy-duty ziplock plastic bag with a very small opening cut in one corner of the bag. Pipe 1-inch mounds, about 1 tablespoon each, onto prepared cookie sheets, spacing them about 2 inches apart. Lift cookie sheets and sharply rap them once or twice on the countertop to slightly flatten mounds of batter. This technique helps to create the distinctive macaroon edge (*pied*) during baking.

Bake until firm to touch and tops are shiny but not cracked, about 15 to 18 minutes. Cool completely on cookie sheets placed on wire racks.

For the filling: In a small saucepan, heat cream until it simmers slightly. Remove from heat and whisk in chopped chocolate. Stir until smooth and mixture begins to thicken.

On the flat side of half the cookies, spread ½ teaspoon of filling. Place a second cookie, flat side down, on top of filling and gently press cookies together.

Store cookies in an airtight container for up to 3 days, or refrigerate for longer shelf life.

Baker's Note: Stand the pastry bag in a tall glass while filling it with batter or when not in use.

Pecan Wedding Cakes

MAKES 24 TO 30 COOKIES

Wedding cakes, sometimes called tea cakes, can be found on cookie tables at traditional Eastern European weddings. These delicate pecan cookies are a gluten-free version of cookies my mom made for me as a child. Their light, crumbly texture and buttery, pecan flavor make them a great addition to a holiday cookie platter.

⅔ cup brown rice flour

3 tablespoons potato starch

1 tablespoon plus 2 teaspoons tapioca flour

¼ teaspoon xanthan gum

¼ cup almond flour

8 tablespoons (1 stick) unsalted butter, room temperature

2 tablespoons powdered sugar, plus extra for dusting

½ teaspoon pure vanilla extract

½ tablespoon water

⅛ teaspoon fine grain sea salt

1 cup finely chopped pecans

In a medium bowl, sift together brown rice flour, potato starch, tapioca flour, and xanthan gum. Whisk in almond flour. Set aside.

In the large bowl of an electric mixer, with mixer speed set to medium, cream butter, about 1 to 2 minutes. Add powdered sugar, vanilla extract, water, and salt. Beat until well combined. Reduce mixer speed to low. Add flour mixture and pecans. Mix until thoroughly incorporated. Chill in a covered bowl, for 1 to 2 hours, or overnight.

Preheat oven to 350°F. Line cookie sheets with parchment.

Using a small cookie scoop, form dough into 1-inch balls. Space them about 1 inch apart on prepared cookie sheets. Bake until bottoms are light brown and tops are pale golden brown, about 12 to 15 minutes. Cool for 5 minutes on cookie sheets, and while still warm, sift a generous amount of powdered sugar over cookies. Transfer cookies, still on parchment, to wire racks to cool completely. Dust with more powdered sugar before serving.

Store cookies in an airtight container for up to 5 days, layered between sheets of parchment or wax paper.

Baker's Note: For an extra sweet cookie, roll the cookies in powdered sugar just before serving.

Chocolate Peppermint Cookies

These yummy peppermint cookies are crunchy on the outside and fudgy on the inside. If you are a fan of chocolate and peppermint, these will be on your must-make list.

1½ cups powdered sugar

⅔ cup Dutch-process cocoa

2 large egg whites

⅛ teaspoon salt

½ teaspoon pure vanilla extract

½ teaspoon pure peppermint extract

½ cup mini chocolate chips

Preheat oven to 350°F. Line cookie sheets with parchment.

In a medium bowl, sift together the powdered sugar and cocoa. Set aside.

In the small bowl of an electric mixer, combine egg whites and salt. Set mixer speed to high and beat until soft peaks form. Add sugar-cocoa mixture, 1 tablespoon at a time, until thoroughly combined. Set mixer speed to low. Mix in vanilla and peppermint extracts. Add chocolate chips and mix until thoroughly combined. Dough will have consistency of thick frosting.

Using a small cookie scoop, shape dough into 1-inch mounds and drop onto prepared cookie sheets, spacing them about 2 inches apart. Bake until tops are shiny and faintly cracked, about 10 to 12 minutes. Cool completely on cookie sheets placed on wire racks.

Store cookies in an airtight container for up to 5 days.

Almond Hazelnut Cookies

I love the taste of toasted almonds and hazelnuts in this light, chewy, macaroon-like cookie. They are great plain or rolled in granulated sugar.

1 large egg, separated

½ cup sugar, plus extra for rolling

¼ teaspoon salt

¼ teaspoon pure vanilla extract

¼ cup plus 2 tablespoons finely ground toasted hazelnuts

¼ cup plus 2 tablespoons finely ground toasted whole almonds

¼ teaspoon cream of tartar

Preheat oven to 300°F. Line cookie sheets with parchment.

In the small bowl of an electric mixer, with speed set to medium, beat egg yolk until pale yellow. Gradually add ½ cup sugar and beat until combined. Add salt and vanilla extract and beat until combined. Set mixer speed to low. Add hazelnuts and almonds, and mix until thoroughly combined. Transfer mixture to another bowl. Set aside.

Clean bowl and blades of electric mixer.

In the cleaned small bowl, with the mixer's speed set to high, beat egg white until foamy. Add cream of tartar and beat until soft peaks form. Turn off mixer and, using a rubber spatula, carefully fold in nut mixture.

Using a small cookie scoop, shape dough into 1-inch balls. Roll balls in granulated sugar, if desired. Space cookies 2 inches apart on prepared cookie sheets. Bake until pale golden brown, about 15 to 18 minutes. Transfer cookies, still on parchment, to wire racks to cool completely.

Store cookies in an airtight container for up to 1 week.

Chocolate Orange Crunchies

MAKES 12 TO 18 COOKIES

These crunchy, no-bake cookies resemble chocolate confections in taste and texture. Crystallized ginger makes a great substitute for the candied orange peel, if you prefer something spicy.

½ cup finely chopped toasted whole almonds

2 tablespoons finely chopped unsalted natural pistachios

2½ tablespoons finely chopped candied orange peel

½ cup gluten-free crisp rice cereal

4½ ounces bittersweet chocolate, chopped (use only high-quality, gluten-free chocolate)

Line a cookie sheet with parchment.

In a medium bowl, combine almonds, pistachios, orange peel, and rice cereal.

In the top of a double boiler, set over simmering water, melt chocolate.

Pour melted chocolate over nut-rice mixture, and mix until combined.

Using a medium cookie scoop, drop double tablespoons of mixture onto prepared cookie sheet, spacing them 1½ inches apart. Refrigerate until set, about 20 minutes.

Store cookies in an airtight container for up to 1 week, layered between sheets of parchment or wax paper.

Baker's Note: Use high quality, gluten-free chocolate to get a rich chocolate taste.

Walnut Citrus Cookies

MAKES 48 TO 60 COOKIES

These dense, chewy walnut cookies have a citrus overtone. The flavor is reminiscent of a holiday cookie that friends from Eastern Europe shared with my family when I was a child.

⅔ cup brown rice flour

3 tablespoons potato starch

1 tablespoon plus 2 teaspoons
   tapioca flour

¼ teaspoon xanthan gum

½ teaspoon salt

¼ cup almond flour

1½ cups lightly toasted walnuts,
   plus ½ cup for rolling

1 cup granulated sugar,
   plus 2 tablespoons for rolling

8 tablespoons (1 stick) unsalted butter,
   room temperature

2 large eggs

1 teaspoon grated lemon zest

1 teaspoon grated orange zest

1 teaspoon pure vanilla extract

In a medium bowl, sift together brown rice flour, potato starch, tapioca flour, xanthan gum, and salt. Whisk in almond flour. Set aside.

In the large bowl of a food processor, pulse 1½ cups of walnuts until finely ground. Set aside.

In the large bowl of an electric mixer, combine butter and 1 cup sugar. Set mixer speed to high. Beat until light and fluffy, about 1 to 2 minutes. Add eggs and beat for another 1 to 2 minutes. Add lemon and orange zests and vanilla extract. Beat until combined. Reduce mixer speed to low. Add flour mixture and mix until combined. Add ground walnuts and mix until combined. Chill in a covered bowl overnight.

Preheat oven to 350°F. Line cookie sheets with parchment.

Chop remaining ½ cup toasted walnuts. Put in a small bowl and mix with 2 tablespoons sugar.

Using a small cookie scoop, shape dough into 1-inch balls. Roll balls in walnut-sugar mixture and place on prepared cookie sheets, spacing them about 2 inches apart. Bake until bottoms are golden brown, about 12 to 15 minutes. Cool on cookie sheets for 2 minutes. Transfer cookies, still on parchment, to wire racks to cool completely.

Store cookies in an airtight container for up to 5 days.

Five-Spice Ginger Cookies

These chewy, gingery cookies have a light and delicate texture. The combination of Chinese five-spice powder and crystallized ginger makes them spicy and aromatic. They are great on their own, or served with a dish of fruit or a bowl of vanilla ice cream.

⅔ cup brown rice flour

3 tablespoons potato starch

1 tablespoon plus 2 teaspoons tapioca flour

½ teaspoon baking soda

¼ teaspoon xanthan gum

¼ teaspoon fine grain sea salt

1 teaspoon five-spice powder

¼ cup almond flour

1½ tablespoons finely chopped crystallized ginger

2 tablespoons granulated sugar

8 tablespoons (1 stick) unsalted butter, melted and cooled

½ cup packed light brown sugar

1 large egg

In a medium bowl, sift together brown rice flour, potato starch, tapioca flour, baking soda, xanthan gum, sea salt, and five-spice powder. Whisk in almond flour. Set aside.

In the small bowl of a food processor, pulse crystallized ginger and granulated sugar until finely ground.

In the large bowl of an electric mixer, combine ginger-sugar mixture, melted butter, and light brown sugar. Set mixer speed to high and beat until combined, about 2 to 3 minutes. Add egg and beat until combined, about 1 to 2 minutes. Reduce mixer speed to low. Add flour mixture and mix until just incorporated. Divide dough into quarters and wrap each quarter in plastic wrap or wax paper. Chill for at least 8 hours, to allow flavors to develop.

Preheat oven to 350°F. Line cookie sheets with parchment.

Roll dough, one quarter at a time, between sheets of wax paper, to ¼-inch thickness. Cut with 1-inch round cookie cutter, dipping cookie cutter in brown rice flour or all-purpose gluten-free flour to aid cutting. Place cookies on prepared cookie sheets, spacing them about 2½ inches apart. If dough becomes too soft to reroll easily, return it to the refrigerator or place it in the freezer for 5 to 10 minutes, until it is firm enough to reroll. Bake until cookies puff and turn a shade darker, about 8 to 10 minutes. Cool on cookie sheets for 5 minutes. Transfer cookies, still on parchment, to wire racks to cool completely.

Store cookies in an airtight container for up to 5 days, layered between sheets of parchment or wax paper.

Double-Chocolate and Double-Hazelnut Biscotti

MAKES 30 TO 36 COOKIES

Toasted hazelnuts, Dutch-process cocoa, and dark chocolate combine to make this delicious double-chocolate, double-hazelnut sensation. For a "triple-double," dip cookies in melted chocolate, and watch your fans go wild.

1 cup brown rice flour

⅓ cup potato starch

2½ tablespoons tapioca flour

½ teaspoon baking powder

½ teaspoon baking soda

½ teaspoon xanthan gum

¼ teaspoon salt

½ cup Dutch-process cocoa

2 teaspoons instant espresso powder

¼ cup plus 2 tablespoons almond flour

¼ cup finely ground, lightly-toasted hazelnuts

1 cup granulated sugar

3 ounces bittersweet or semisweet chocolate, chopped

8 tablespoons (1 stick) unsalted butter, room temperature

1 teaspoon pure vanilla extract

1 teaspoon pure almond extract

2 large eggs

1 cup coarsely chopped, lightly-toasted hazelnuts

In a medium bowl, sift together brown rice flour, potato starch, tapioca flour, baking powder, baking soda, xanthan gum, salt, Dutch-process cocoa, and espresso powder. Whisk in almond flour and finely ground hazelnuts. Set aside.

In the large bowl of a food processor, combine sugar and chocolate. Pulse until chocolate is finely chopped. Set aside.

In the large bowl of an electric mixer, with mixer speed set to high, cream butter until light and fluffy, about 1 to 2 minutes. Add sugar-chocolate mixture. Beat until fluffy, about 2 to 3 minutes. Add vanilla and almond extracts. Beat until combined. Add eggs, one at a time, and beat until light and fluffy, about 2 minutes. Reduce mixer speed to low. Add flour mixture and mix until just incorporated. Mix in coarsely chopped hazelnuts. Chill in a covered bowl, for 1 to 2 hours, or overnight.

Preheat oven to 350°F. Line cookie sheet with parchment.

Divide dough in half. Working with one half at a time, place dough on a sheet of wax paper and roll into a smooth log 2 inches in diameter and about 10 inches long. Place both logs on cookie sheet, spacing well apart. Bake until firm to touch, about 30 to 35 minutes. Cool on cookie sheet 15 minutes.

Carefully transfer the logs to a work area. With a serrated knife, cut logs crosswise into slices about ½ inch thick.

Lay the slices flat on cool, parchment-lined cookie sheets, and bake for another 10 to 12 minutes. Transfer cookies, still on parchment, to wire racks to cool completely.

Store cookies in an airtight container for up to 1 week.

Baker's Note: For a really indulgent treat, melt 6 ounces of bittersweet chocolate in the top of a double boiler. Dip one side of each cookie in the melted chocolate. Gently shake off excess chocolate and dry on a wire rack with chocolate side up.

Pine Nut Cookies

MAKES 36 TO 48 COOKIES

My girlfriend Angela makes the best pine nut cookies. They are light and chewy with a crunchy nut top, and they're a favorite at family gatherings. This adaptation uses ground pine nuts to replace wheat flour. I use Solo almond paste, as it is the only one I have found that is gluten-free.

8 ounces gluten-free almond paste, cut into small pieces

½ cup granulated sugar

½ cup powdered sugar

½ teaspoon pure vanilla extract

1½ cups lightly toasted pine nuts

2 large egg whites

1 teaspoon baking powder

pinch salt

Preheat oven to 350°F. Line cookie sheets with parchment.

In the large bowl of a food processor, combine almond paste, granulated sugar, powdered sugar, vanilla extract, and 3 tablespoons of toasted pine nuts. Pulse until mixture resembles coarse crumbs. Add egg whites, baking powder, and salt. Pulse until completely incorporated. Dough will be very soft.

Drop rounded half tablespoons of dough onto prepared cookie sheets, spacing them about 2½ inches apart. Sprinkle 1 teaspoon of pine nuts on top of each cookie, and gently press with fingers to adhere. Bake until pale golden brown, about 12 to 14 minutes. Transfer cookies, still on parchment, to wire racks to cool completely.

Store cookies in an airtight container for up to 5 days.

Sources for Ingredients

Gluten-free baking products, such as brown rice flour, tapioca flour, and xanthan gum, can be found in the organic section of many grocery stores, health food stores, organic markets, or online. The list of ingredient sources below is not exhaustive, but it is an excellent reference guide to get started.

Allergy Grocer, LLC
Miss Roben's
7135 Minstrel Way, Suite 101
Columbia, MD 21045
888-476-3350
www.allergygrocer.com
Gluten-free flours, baking supplies, and prepared foods

Amazon.com
1200 12th Ave. S., Suite 1200
Seattle, WA 98144
www.amazon.com
Gluten-free flours, baking supplies, and prepared foods

American Spoon Foods, Inc.
P.O. Box 566
Petoskey, MI 49770
800-222-5886
www.spoon.com
Dried fruits, nuts, and jams

Arrowhead Mills
4600 Sleepytime Drive
Boulder, CO 80301
800-434-4246
www.arrowheadmills.com
Gluten-free flours

Authentic Foods
1850 West 169th Street, Suite B
Gardena, CA 90247
800-806-4737
www.authenticfoods.com
Gluten-free flours, baking supplies, and prepared foods

Bickford Flavors
19007 St. Clair Avenue
Cleveland, OH 44117
800-283-8322
www.bickfordflavors.com
Gluten-free extracts

Bob's Red Mill Whole Grain Store
5000 SE International Way
Milwaukie, OR 97222
800-349-2173
www.bobsredmill.com
Gluten-free flours and other baking supplies

Boyajian Incorporated
144 Will Drive
Canton, MA 02021
800-965-0665
www.boyajianinc.com
Gluten-free extracts

Chukar Cherries Company
P.O. Box 510
Prosser, WA 99350
800-624-9544
www.chukar.com
Dried fruits and jams

Ener-G Foods, Inc.
5960 First Avenue South
P.O. Box 84487
Seattle, WA 98124
800-331-5222
www.ener-g.com
Gluten-free baking supplies

Gluten-Free Mall
4927 Sonoma Highway, Suite C1
Santa Rosa, CA 95409
866-575-3720
www.glutenfreemall.com
Gluten-free flours, baking supplies, and prepared foods

Gluten-Free Pantry
P.O. Box 840
Glastonbury, CT 06033
800-291-8386
www.glutenfree.com
Gluten-free flours, baking supplies, and prepared foods

Gluten Solutions, Inc.
206 E Ave. 32
Los Angeles, CA 90031
877-747-7565
www.glutensolutions.com
Gluten-free flours, baking supplies, and prepared foods

King Arthur Flour Company
135 Route 5 South
Norwich, VT 05055
800-827-6836
www.kingarthurflour.com
Gluten-free flours and baking supplies

Kinnikinnick Foods
10306-112 Street
Edmonton, Alberta T5K 1N1, Canada
877-503-4466
www.kinnikinnick.com
Gluten-free flours and baking supplies

NutsOnline.com
125 Moen St.
Cranford, NJ 07016
800-558-6887
www.nutsonline.com
Dried fruits and nuts

TIC Gums
4609 Richlynn Drive
Belcamp, MD 21017
800-899-3953
www.ticgums.com
Gluten-free baking gums

Tom Sawyer's Gluten Free Products
2155 West State Route 89A, Suite 106
Sedona, AZ 86336
877-372-8800
www.glutenfreeflour.com
Gluten-free all-purpose flour and oats

Resources for Celiac Disease

There are many information sources on gluten-free diets, celiac disease, and wheat allergies. Most sources are credible, but sometimes you will find conflicting information. Compare sources, look for credentials, and seek the most recent information. Below are some of the magazines and support groups that I found while writing this book. New studies and books are published frequently, and can be found by doing a simple Internet search. This list is not exhaustive, but it provides a good starting point.

NEWSLETTERS AND MAGAZINES

Gluten-Free Living
P.O. Box 375, Maple Shade, NJ 08052
800-324-8781
www.glutenfreeliving.com
Magazine

Journal of Gluten Sensitivity
4927 Sonoma Hwy., Ste C
Santa Rosa, CA 95409
Tel: 707-509-4528
www.celiac.com
Newsletter and Web site

Living Without
P.O. Box 420234
Palm Coast, FL 32142
800-474-8614
www.livingwithout.com
Magazine, newsletter, and Web site

INFORMATION SOURCES AND ADVOCACY GROUPS

American Celiac Disease Alliance
2504 Duxbury Place
Alexandria, VA 22308
703-622-3331
www.americanceliac.org
Information and advocacy

Celiac Disease Center at Columbia University
Harkness Pavilion
180 Fort Washington Ave. #934
New York, NY 10032
212-342-4529 or cb2280@columbia.edu
www.celiacdiseasecenter.org
Information and advocacy

Celiac Disease Foundation
13251 Ventura Blvd. #1
Studio City, CA 91604
818-990-2354
www.celiac.org
Information and advocacy

Celiac Sprue Association
P.O. Box 31700
Omaha, NE 68131
877-272-4272
www.csaceliacs.org
Information resource and support group

GFCF Diet Support Group Information Website
P.O. Box 1692
Palm Harbor, FL 34682
www.gfcfdiet.com
Support group

Gluten Intolerance Group (GIG)
31214 124th Ave. SE
Auburn, WA 98092
253-833-6655
www.gluten.net
Information and advocacy

National Foundation for Celiac Awareness
P.O. Box 544
Ambler, PA 19002
215-325-1306
www.celiaccentral.org
Support group

Raising Our Celiac Kids (R.O.C.K.)
www.celiackids.com
Support group

Index

agave nectar, 9
almond butter instead of peanut butter, 61
almond flour, 8
   recommended gluten-free flour mix, 15–17
almonds
   Almond Hazelnut Cookies, 127
   Almond Lemon Biscotti, 39
   almond paste in Pine Nut Cookies, 136
   Chocolate Almond Dreams, 117
   Chocolate Orange Crunchies, 128
   Chocolate Raspberry Fingers, 99
   Double-Cherry Streusel Bars, 96
   French Chocolate Macaroons, 120
   Fruit and Nut Granola Bars, 95
   Krissy's Apple Cookies, 76
   Oatmeal Almond Cookies with Dates, 43
apples in Krissy's Apple Cookies, 76
apricots, dried
   Apricot and Polenta Jewels, 67
   Fruit and Nut Granola Bars, 95
   Krissy's Apple Cookies, 76

baking pans, 19, 20, 21. See also cookie sheets;
   parchment paper, use of
baking powder, 9
baking soda, 9
Banana Bites, 64
bar cookies
   Chocolate Orange Bars with Hazelnuts, 92
   Chocolate Raspberry Fingers, 99
   Double-Cherry Streusel Bars, 96
   Double-Chocolate Brownies with Walnuts, 84
   Fruit and Nut Granola Bars, 95
   Lemon Squares, 91
   Macadamia Nut Blondies, 87
   Rocky Road S'Mores Bars, 88
barley flour, 12
biscotti
   Almond Lemon Biscotti, 39
   Double-Chocolate and Double-Hazelnut
      Biscotti, 135
blueberries, dried in Double-Berry Meringues, 110
Blueberry Jam Sandwiches, 80
Bob's Red Mill, 6, 15
brown rice flour, 6, 8, 9
   recommended gluten-free flour mix, 15–17
brown sugar. See sugar, brown
Browned Butter Frosting, 79

brownie cutter, 21–22

cakelike cookies, 16
   Double-Chocolate Brownies with Walnuts, 84
   Frosted Pumpkin Currant Spice Cookies, 79
candies. See cookie decorations
cashew butter instead of peanut butter, 31
celebration cookies
   Almond Hazelnut Cookies, 127
   Chocolate Orange Crunchies, 128
   Chocolate Peppermint Cookies, 124
   Cranberry-Orange-Nut Drops, 72
   Double-Chocolate and Double-Hazelnut
      Biscotti, 135
   Five-Spice Ginger Cookies, 132
   French Chocolate Macaroons, 120
   Frosted Pumpkin Currant Spice Cookies, 79
   Pecan Wedding Cakes, 123
   Pine Nut Cookies, 136
   Walnut Citrus Cookies, 131
Celiac Disease: A Hidden Epidemic (Green and
   Jones), 4
celiac disease as an autoimmune disease, 4
Celiac Disease Center at Columbia University, 4
Celiac Sprue Association, 7
cherries, dried
   Double-Berry Meringues, 110
   Double-Cherry Streusel Bars, 96
   Matt's No-Bake Chocolate Cherry Crispies, 58
chilling dough, 19
chocolate, 10, 20. See also cocoa powder
   bittersweet chocolate, gluten-free
      Chocolate Orange Crunchies, 128
      Double-Chocolate and Double-Hazelnut
         Biscotti, 135
   chocolate chips
      Chocolate Almond Dreams, 117
      Chocolate Chip and Pecan Cookies, 28
      Chocolate Chip Raspberry Meringues, 106
      Chocolate Peppermint Cookies, 124
      Chocolate Raspberry Fingers, 99
      Coconut Surprises, 75
      Double-Chocolate Brownies with Walnuts,
         84
      Double-Chocolate Pizza Cookie, 50
      Fudge-Filled Drops, 105
      ganache filling for French Chocolate
         Macaroons, 120

   Matt's No-Bake Chocolate Cherry Crispies,
      58
   No-Bake Chocolate Oatmeal Drops, 54
   Rocky Road S'Mores Bars, 88
   for topping of Double-Chocolate Pizza
      Cookie, 50
   Vanilla Bean Cookies, 32
unsweetened chocolate
   Chocolate Orange Bars with Hazelnuts, 92
   Double-Chocolate Brownies with Walnuts,
      84
white chocolate, gluten-free in Macadamia Nut
   Blondies, 87
cinnamon in Sweet Cinnamon Snickerdoodles, 53
citrus zest and zesting, 19, 21, 23
   lemon zest
      Almond Lemon Biscotti, 39
      Blueberry Jam Sandwiches, 80
      Lemon Drops, 68
      Lemon Squares, 91
   orange zest
      Chocolate Orange Bars with Hazelnuts, 92
      Cranberry-Orange-Nut Drops, 72
      Ginger Molasses Cookies, 36
   Walnut Citrus Cookies, 131
cocoa powder, 10. See also chocolate
   Dutch-process cocoa
      Chocolate Peanut Butter Cups, 61
      Chocolate Peppermint Cookies, 124
      Double-Chocolate and Double-Hazelnut
         Biscotti, 135
      Double-Chocolate Pizza Cookie, 50
      French Chocolate Macaroons, 120
   not Dutch-process cocoa in Chocolate
      Raspberry Fingers, 99
coconut
   Banana Bites, 64
   Coconut Surprises, 75
   Date Walnut Logs, 71
   Double-Cherry Streusel Bars, 96
   Fruit and Nut Granola Bars, 95
   Krissy's Apple Cookies, 76
colored sugars. See decorated cookies
confectioner's sugar. See sugar, powdered
cookie cutter cookies. See rolled cookies
cookie cutters, 22
cookie decorations. See decorated cookies
cookie scoops, 22

cookie sheets, 22. *See also* baking pans
corn syrup, 10
    Fruit and Nut Granola Bars, 95
cornmeal, 8
    Apricot and Polenta Jewels, 67
cornstarch (cornflour), 8, 9, 10, 13
    Lemon Drops, 68
    Lemon Squares, 91
    Vanilla Bean Cookies, 32
cranberries, dried
    Cranberry-Orange-Nut Drops, 72
    Fruit and Nut Granola Bars, 95
cream, heavy
    Browned Butter Frosting, 79
    ganache filling for French Chocolate
      Macaroons, 120
    Gingerbread Cookies, 57
    Rocky Road S'Mores Bars, 88
cream cheese in Double-Chocolate Pizza
  Cookie, 50
cream of tartar, 9
creaming technique, 19
currants in Frosted Pumpkin Currant Spice
  Cookies, 79
cutting in technique, 19, 23

dairy products, gluten-free, 11
dates
    Banana Bites, 64
    Date Walnut Logs, 71
    Fruit and Nut Bonbons, 114
    Oatmeal Almond Cookies with Dates, 43
decorated cookies
    Decorated Cookie Cutouts, 49
    decorating techniques and tips, 7, 12, 20, 24–25
    Double-Chocolate Pizza Cookie, 50
    Gingerbread Cookies, 57
    Old-Fashioned Sugar Cookies, 40
double boiler, 20, 22
Double-Berry Meringues, 110
Double-Cherry Streusel Bars, 96
Double-Chocolate and Double-Hazelnut Biscotti,
  135
Double-Chocolate Brownies with Walnuts, 84
Double-Chocolate Pizza Cookie, 50
drop cookies. *See also* egg whites, meringues
    Banana Bites, 64
    Chocolate Chip and Pecan Cookies, 28
    Chocolate Orange Crunchies, 128
    Chocolate Peanut Butter Cups, 61
    Chocolate Peppermint Cookies, 124

    Flourless Peanut Butter Cookies, 31
    Frosted Pumpkin Currant Spice Cookies, 79
    Ginger Molasses Cookies, 36
    Jam Thumbprints, 46
    Krissy's Apple Cookies, 76
    Lemon Drops, 68
    Matt's No-Bake Chocolate Cherry Crispies, 58
    No-Bake Chocolate Oatmeal Drops, 54
    Oatmeal Almond Cookies with Dates, 43
    Pecan Wedding Cakes, 123
    Sweet Cinnamon Snickerdoodles, 53
    Vanilla Bean Cookies, 32
dry measuring cups and spoons, 22
dusting pans, 19

egg whites, 9, 19, 20
    Almond Hazelnut Cookies, 127
    Chocolate Peanut Butter Cups, 61
    Chocolate Peppermint Cookies, 124
    Chocolate Raspberry Fingers, 99
    Coconut Surprises, 75
    French Chocolate Macaroons, 120
    meringues
        Brown Sugar Pecan Kisses, 102
        Chocolate Almond Dreams, 117
        Chocolate Chip Raspberry Meringues, 106
        Double-Berry Meringues, 110
        Fruit and Nut Bonbons, 114
        Fudge-Filled Drops, 105
        Hazelnut Meringues, 109
        Lavender Clouds, 113
    Royal Icing Using Egg Whites, 24
egg yolks, 9
    Almond Hazelnut Cookies, 127
    Blueberry Jam Sandwiches, 80
    Fudge-Filled Drops, 105
eggs, tips and techniques, 9, 19, 20
electric mixer, 22
equipment used in baking cookies, 21–23
espresso powder, 10
    Double-Chocolate and Double-Hazelnut
      Biscotti, 135
extracts. *See* flavorings, gluten-free

figs, dried in Fruit and Nut Bonbons, 114
firm to touch definition, 19
Five-Spice Ginger Cookies, 132
flavorings, gluten-free, 10–11. *See also* chocolate;
  cocoa powder; espresso powder; vanilla beans
flour, gluten-free, 8
    flours to avoid, 4, 12

    grinding nut flours, 20
    recommended gluten-free flour mix, 15–17
flourless cookies. *See also* eggwhites, meringues
    Almond Hazelnut Cookies, 127
    Banana Bites, 64
    Chocolate Orange Crunchies, 128
    Coconut Surprises, 75
    Date Walnut Logs, 71
    Flourless Peanut Butter Cookies, 31
      alternate recipe in Baker's Note, 61
    French Chocolate Macaroons, 120
    Fruit and Nut Granola Bars, 95
    Krissy's Apple Cookies, 76
    Matt's No-Bake Chocolate Cherry Crispies, 58
    No-Bake Chocolate Oatmeal Drops, 54
    Pine Nut Cookies, 136
    Vanilla Bean Cookies, 32
flours to avoid, 4, 12
folding in technique, 20
food processor, 22
French Chocolate Macaroons, 120
Frosting, Browned Butter, 79
fruit cookies
    Apricot and Polenta Jewels, 67
    Banana Bites, 64
    Blueberry Jam Sandwiches, 80
    Chocolate Orange Bars with Hazelnuts, 92
    Chocolate Orange Crunchies, 128
    Chocolate Raspberry Fingers, 99
    Coconut Surprises, 75
    Cranberry-Orange-Nut Drops, 72
    Date Walnut Logs, 71
    Double-Berry Meringues, 110
    Double-Cherry Streusel Bars, 96
    Fruit and Nut Bonbons, 114
    Fruit and Nut Granola Bars, 95
    Krissy's Apple Cookies, 76
    Lemon Drops, 68
    Lemon Squares, 91
    Matt's No-Bake Chocolate Cherry Crispies, 58
    Oatmeal Almond Cookies with Dates, 43
    Walnut Citrus Cookies, 131
fruits, gluten-free, 11
Fudge-Filled Drops, 105

ganache filling for French Chocolate Macaroons,
  120
gelatin powder, gluten-free, 11
    Chocolate Chip Raspberry Meringues, 106
ginger, crystallized in Walnut Citrus Cookies, 132
Ginger Molasses Cookies, 36

Gingerbread Cookies, 57
gluten, 4, 6–8
    gluten contamination, 4, 6, 14
gluten-free cooking
    creating the baking environment for, 14, 18, 21
    gluten-free ingredients, 6–13
graham crackers, gluten-free in Rocky Road
   S'Mores Bars, 88
greasing pans, 20
Green, Peter H. R., 4
guar gum, 6, 8, 9

hazelnut flour, 8
hazelnuts
    Almond Hazelnut Cookies, 127
    Blueberry Jam Sandwiches, 80
    Chocolate Orange Bars with Hazelnuts, 92
    Double-Chocolate and Double-Hazelnut
     Biscotti, 135
    Hazelnut Meringues, 109
holiday cookies. *See* celebration cookies
honey, 10
    Frosted Pumpkin Currant Spice Cookies, 79
    Krissy's Apple Cookies, 76

ingredients, gluten-free, 6–13

jams and preserves
    blueberry jam in Blueberry Jam Sandwiches, 80
    cherry preserves in Double-Cherry Streusel
     Bars, 96
    Jam Thumbprints, 46
    raspberry jam in Chocolate Raspberry Fingers,
     99

knives, 22
Krissy's Apple Cookies, 76

labels, reading, 7, 12
Lavender Clouds, 113
leaveners, gluten-free, 9–10
lemon oil in Lemon Drops, 68
lemons (juice or zest)
    Almond Lemon Biscotti, 39
    Blueberry Jam Sandwiches, 80
    Double-Cherry Streusel Bars, 96
    Lemon Drops, 68
    Lemon Squares, 91
    Walnut Citrus Cookies, 131
liquid measuring cups and spoons, 22–23

Macadamia Nut Blondies, 87
macaroons
    Coconut Surprises, 75
    French Chocolate Macaroons, 120
manioc flour. *See* tapioca flour
maple syrup, 10
    Fruit and Nut Granola Bars, 95
marshmallows, gluten-free in Rocky Road S'Mores
   Bars, 88
Master Recipes for Royal Icing
    Using Egg Whites, 24
    Using Meringue Powder, 24
Matt's No-Bake Chocolate Cherry Crispies, 58
measuring techniques, 19, 20, 22–23
meringue powder in Royal Icing Using Meringue
   Powder, 24
meringues. *See* egg whites, meringues
mixing bowls, 23
molasses, 10
    Ginger Molasses Cookies, 36
    Gingerbread Cookies, 57

New Oxford Book of Food Plants, The (Vaughan and
   Geissler), 12
no-bake cookies
    Chocolate Orange Crunchies, 128
    Matt's No-Bake Chocolate Cherry Crispies, 58
    No-Bake Chocolate Oatmeal Drops, 54
nut flours, grinding of, 20
nuts, 11, 19, 21, 24

Oatmeal Almond Cookies with Dates, 43
oils and shortenings, gluten-free, 11
Old-Fashioned Sugar Cookies, 40
orange peel, candied in Chocolate Orange
   Crunchies, 128
oranges (juice or zest)
    Chocolate Orange Bars with Hazelnuts, 92
    Cranberry-Orange-Nut Drops, 72
    Ginger Molasses Cookies, 36
    Walnut Citrus Cookies, 131
oven, preheating, 20

pans for baking, 20
pans for baking, tips and techniques, 19
parchment paper, use of, 14, 18, 21, 23
pastry bag and tips, 20, 23, 120
pastry cutter, 23
peanuts and peanut butter, 11
    and allergies, 7, 31, 61
    Chocolate Peanut Butter Cups, 61

Flourless Peanut Butter Cookies, 31
pecans
    Brown Sugar Pecan Kisses, 102
    Chocolate Chip and Pecan Cookies, 28
    Pecan Wedding Cakes, 123
Peppermint Cookies, Chocolate, 124
Pine Nut Cookies, 136
piped cookies: French Chocolate Macaroons, 120
piping technique. *See* pastry bag and tips
pistachios
    Chocolate Orange Crunchies, 128
    Cranberry-Orange-Nut Drops, 72
    Fudge-Filled Drops, 105
polenta. *See* cornmeal
potato starch, 8
    recommended gluten-free flour mix, 15–17
powdered sugar. *See* sugar, powdered
preheating oven, 20
preserves. *See* jams and preserves
pumpkin puree in Frosted Pumpkin Currant Spice
   Cookies, 79
pumpkin seeds (pepitas) in Fruit and Nut Granola
   Bars, 95

raspberry gelatin powder in Chocolate Chip
   Raspberry Meringues, 106
raspberry jam in Chocolate Raspberry Fingers, 99
rice cereal, gluten-free
    Chocolate Orange Crunchies, 128
    Matt's No-Bake Chocolate Cherry Crispies, 58
rice flour, 6, 8–9
    recommended gluten-free flour mix, 15–17
Rocky Road S'Mores Bars, 88
rolled cookies
    Blueberry Jam Sandwiches, 80
    Decorated Cookie Cutouts, 49
    Gingerbread Cookies, 57
    Shortbread Galettes, 35
    Walnut Citrus Cookies, 132
rolled oats, gluten-free
    Banana Bites, 64
    Fruit and Nut Granola Bars, 95
    No-Bake Chocolate Oatmeal Drops, 54
    Oatmeal Almond Cookies with Dates, 43
rolling pin, 23
room temperature, 19, 20
Royal Icing
    recipes for, 24
    used on Decorated Cookie Cutouts, 49
    used on Gingerbread Cookies, 57
rye flour, 12

sandwich cookies
    Blueberry Jam Sandwiches, 80
    French Chocolate Macaroons, 120
Scandinavian Journal of Gastroenterology, 12
seeds, gluten-free, 11
Shortbread Galettes, 35
shortening. *See vegetable shortening*
sifters and sifting technique, 20–21, 23
sliced cookies
    Almond Lemon Biscotti, 39
    Apricot and Polenta Jewels, 67
    Double-Chocolate and Double-Hazelnut
      Biscotti, 135
Snickerdoodles, Sweet Cinnamon, 53
spatulas, 23
spoons, 22
sugar, brown, 9–10
    Brown Sugar Pecan Kisses, 102
    Chocolate Chip and Pecan Cookies, 28
    Chocolate Orange Bars with Hazelnuts, 92
    Cranberry-Orange-Nut Drops, 72
    Date Walnut Logs, 71
    Double-Chocolate Pizza Cookie, 50
    French Chocolate Macaroons, 120
    Fruit and Nut Granola Bars, 95
    Ginger Molasses Cookies, 36
    Gingerbread Cookies, 57
    Macadamia Nut Blondies, 87
    measuring, 19
    Oatmeal Almond Cookies with Dates, 43
    Rocky Road S'Mores Bars, 88
    Walnut Citrus Cookies, 132
sugar, granulated, 10
    Almond Hazelnut Cookies, 127
    Almond Lemon Biscotti, 39
    Apricot and Polenta Jewels, 67
    Blueberry Jam Sandwiches, 80
    Chocolate Chip and Pecan Cookies, 28
    Chocolate Peanut Butter Cups, 61
    Chocolate Raspberry Fingers, 99
    colored sugars for decorating See cookie
      decorations
    Decorated Cookie Cutouts, 49
    Double-Cherry Streusel Bars, 96
    Double-Chocolate and Double-Hazelnut
      Biscotti, 135
    Double-Chocolate Brownies with Walnuts, 84
    Double-Chocolate Pizza Cookie, 50
    Flourless Peanut Butter Cookies, 31
    Jam Thumbprints, 46
    Lemon Squares, 91

Oatmeal Almond Cookies with Dates, 43
Old-Fashioned Sugar Cookies, 40
Pine Nut Cookies, 136
Sweet Cinnamon Snickerdoodles, 53
Vanilla Bean Cookies, 32
Walnut Citrus Cookies, 131
sugar, powdered
    Browned Butter Frosting, 79
    Chocolate Peppermint Cookies, 124
    Double-Berry Meringues, 110
    filling for Chocolate Peanut Butter Cups, 61
    French Chocolate Macaroons, 120
    Lavender Clouds, 113
    Lemon Squares, 91
    Pecan Wedding Cakes, 123
    Pine Nut Cookies, 136
    Royal Icing Using Egg Whites, 24
    Royal Icing Using Meringue Powder, 24
    Shortbread Galettes, 35
    for topping of Double-Chocolate Pizza Cookie,
      50
sugar, sanding. *See cookie decorations*
sugar, superfine
    Chocolate Almond Dreams, 117
    Double-Berry Meringues, 110
    French Chocolate Macaroons, 120
    Fruit and Nut Bonbons, 114
    Fudge-Filled Drops, 105
    Hazelnut Meringues, 109
    Lavender Clouds, 113
sunflower seeds in Fruit and Nut Granola Bars, 95
Sweet Cinnamon Snickerdoodles, 53
sweeteners, gluten-free, 9–10

tapioca flour, 6, 9
    recommended gluten-free flour mix, 15–17
techniques and terms in baking, 19–21
thumbprint cookies
    Chocolate Peanut Butter Cups, 61
    Jam Thumbprints, 46
tins for storing cookies, 23

vanilla beans, 11
    Vanilla Bean Cookies, 32
vegetable shortening, 11, 19, 23
vinegar, gluten-free. *See white vinegar*

walnuts
    Date Walnut Logs, 71
    Double-Chocolate Brownies with Walnuts, 84
    Frosted Pumpkin Currant Spice Cookies, 79

Fruit and Nut Bonbons, 114
No-Bake Chocolate Oatmeal Drops, 54
Rocky Road S'Mores Bars, 88
Walnut Citrus Cookies, 131
wax paper, 23
wheat allergies, 5
wheat flour, 12
    equivalent gluten-free flour mix, 17
whisks and whisking, 21, 23
white rice flour, reasons for not using, 9
white vinegar, gluten-free, 12
    Chocolate Chip Raspberry Meringues, 106
wire cooling racks, 23

xanthan gum, 6, 8, 9
    recommended gluten-free flour mix, 15–17

zante currants. *See currants*
zest. *See citrus zest*

ACKNOWLEDGMENTS

As a first-time author, I have many people to thank. It has been quite an adventure getting here. Along the way, I have met some of the most open and generous people I have ever known. Thanks to all of you for making me a member of this very special culinary world.

First, I want to thank all the wonderful people who graciously gave their time and knowledge to me as I wrote my initial proposal. Special thanks to Geoff Cardillo, who connected me to Joanne Smart when the notion of publishing a cookbook was just a random idea. Joanne guided me through the draft of my initial proposal, accepting only a tin of cookies as payment for her help.

Special thanks to author Carliss Retif-Pond for making it clear to me that people would actually be baking my recipes. Thanks also to Shannon Moorman, for connecting me to Carliss.

Many thanks to the dedicated volunteers who baked the test recipes and provided important feedback. Although there were many recipe testers who contributed, the standouts were Laurie Arakawa, Annie Evans, Liz Friedman, Shelby MacLeod, Sumeera Rasul, Ann Swancer, and Karen Zelnick.

I would like to thank my colleagues at R/GA for eating every sample batch of cookies that I baked, providing feedback, and encouraging me to bake, bake, bake. Tim Ayers, Ray Fallon, and Mary Smith deserve special recognition for referring me to copy editors and nutritionists, and for allowing me to observe a professional photo shoot. Special thanks to Stephen Barnwell and Amin Torres for donating their time and photographic skills to create my official portrait. Thanks also to Nick Caro for being the very first to taste every batch of cookies I brought to work, and to Lindsay Kennedy for contributing design ideas to make the gingerbread people special.

Most important, I would like to thank Megan Hiller of Sellers Publishing for plucking my proposal from the "slush pile" of unsolicited submissions. Megan wrote me the nicest rejection and counterproposal that I received. She suggested that I focus on creating gourmet, gluten-free cookies and postpone my original cookbook idea. So here I am.

Thanks also to Stacey Cramp, who has done a fantastic job photographing my cookie creations. It wasn't until she began shooting the cookies that my friends really believed that I was writing a cookbook. Both Megan and Stacey have been great collaborators. Thanks, ladies, for making this real.

And, yes, of course, there are the unwavering men in my life, my wonderful husband, Larry, and my dear friend, Matt. I've never understood how the two of you put up with me. I am just grateful that you do. Thanks for all of your help to make this happen.